CW00551000

CONTENTS

Ships in Focus Publications
Correspondence and editorial:
Roy Fenton
18 Durrington Avenue
London SW20 8NT
020 8879 3527
rfenton@rfenton.demon.co.uk

Orders and photographic:
John & Marion Clarkson
18 Franklands, Longton
Preston PR4 5PD
01772 612855
shipsinfocus@btinternet.com

© 2006 Individual contributors,
John Clarkson and Roy Fenton.

All rights reserved. No part of this publication
may be reproduced, stored in a retrieval system
or transmitted in any form or by any means,
electronic, mechanical, photocopying, recording
or otherwise, without the written permission of
the publisher.

Printed by Amadeus Press Ltd., Cleckheaton,
Yorkshire.
Designed by Hugh Smallwood, John Clarkson
and Roy Fenton.

SHIPS IN FOCUS RECORD
ISBN 1 901703 80 0

SUBSCRIPTION RATES FOR RECORD

Readers can start their subscription with any
issue, and are welcome to backdate it to
receive previous issues.

	3 issues	4 issues
UK	£24	£31
Europe (airmail)	£26	£34
Rest of the world (surface mail)	£26	£34
Rest of the world (airmail)	£31	£41

SHIPS IN FOCUS

July 2006

When a photograph from a Ships in Focus negative appeared in another journal recently, a reader excitedly got in touch with us, as it showed the first ship he had served on and he was anxious for a copy. He had despaired of finding a photograph of her, as his sons had told him it just did not exist, as it could not be found on the Internet.

Naturally, this prompted some musings amongst the editorial team. Yes, there are a lot of photographs on the 'net (and at the risk of sounding like grumpy old men, too many of them reproduced without permission from the copyright holder). But the concept that all known images are out there in cyberspace is a novel one. By inference, the gentleman's son probably believes all human knowledge is out there too.

Much has been said about the Internet liberalising distribution of information, so that everyone who has access to a computer can have their say. At the risk of sounding elitist, however, one must question the value of 'everyone's say' in a context such as shipping history, where a premium is placed on accuracy. Too much of the information seen on maritime history websites is derivative, having been simply copied from other sources, sometimes not even accurately, and often without due acknowledgement to the originator. If it is admitted that the information is provisional, and in some cases derived from hearsay and half-remembered events, as it is for instance on the excellent Norwegian 'Warsailors' website, well and good, but the poor sites damage confidence in the better ones.

As publishers, we would be the first to admit that not everything that appears in books (even ours) is copper-bottomed, sea-going, 100A1, dependable, historical fact. But at least a book has publishers and editors who, one would hope, have made some effort to ascertain whether their authors have done the work themselves and done it well. Publishers have a reputation to maintain, which they should cherish both for its own sake and because it has commercial implications. Most historians and researchers know the authors whose work they can put their faith in, and those they cannot. The Internet is here to stay, and can be a valuable research tool, but its historical content needs to be treated with caution.

John Clarkson   Roy Fenton

July 2006

Booker Venture was Booker Line's first bulk carrier and although designed to carry sugar in bulk she could easily carry other bulk cargoes such as grain when sugar cargoes were not available (see page 70). She is seen here after lengthening in 1966. *[J. & M.Clarkson collection]*

Top: Two near sisters were the *Amakura* (2), completed in 1924 and the *Arakaka* (2) (above) delivered in 1933 and seen here on the Clyde. *[Glasgow University Archives GD320/ 10/1/80/4]*

Middle: After the war two steamers were constructed to replace war losses, the *Arakaka* (3) in 1946 and, right, the *Amakura* (3) in 1949. *[Roy Fenton collection]*

Bottom: The *Booker Courage* at Erskine 28th October 1980, one of three combi-carriers purchased in 1979/80 and all of which were sold in 1983 following a serious slump in trade with Guyana. *[Jim Prentice/ World Ship Society Limited]*

BOOKER LINE

Andrew Bell

It is often forgotten that 2,000 miles of South America's coastline faces north. Towards the western end of this coast, almost adjacent to the Caribbean, are the Guianas which were once divided between Britain, France and Holland. Over the centuries the rich topsoil of the Pakaraika Mountain range has been eroded and washed down rivers by tropical rains, the rivers slowing as they near the equatorial Atlantic with their silt forming rich coastal plains. It was on this bounty of nature that the Europeans, risking disease and hostile tribes, grew that real life El Dorado crop of the 1700 and 1800s, sugar. As late as the 1940s the colony of British Guiana was known as a 'British Sugar Mine'. Acquired from the Dutch in 1796, British Guiana was to remain the only piece of the Empire on the South Atlantic mainland until independent Guyana was created in 1966. So dominant was sugar in the colony's development that it took as a brand name the original name of the land - Demerara.

Bookers and McConnell

As ever trade and the flag were interlinked and early on to the scene in 1815 was Josias Booker of Liverpool managing a cotton plantation and later adding a bankrupt sugar one. The trading business he started began to flourish when he was joined by his brothers George, William and Richard who based themselves in the colony's only large settlement - yet another Georgetown - a name to be found in many British colonies. In 1846 John McConnell arrived together with Josias' son Josias junior, McConnell eventually becoming the senior partner when the Booker family sold out their interests in 1886, the corporate title becoming Booker Brothers, McConnell and Co. in 1900.

Back home on Merseyside other merchants were exploiting two-way trading openings with West Africa, Central America and the Caribbean islands. Many of these merchant venturers were to become vertically integrated: they exported British merchandise in return for tropical crops. Bookers' enterprise was similar to those of John Holt and Lever Brothers, with interests in everything from capital investment in plant in the British colonies, from plantations to insurance services, and from transport infrastructure to agencies for consumer goods. To carry their goods the merchants formed and owned shipping companies which often provoked long, tiring and costly freight rate discounting wars with established lines which were encircled by protective, monopolistic freight conferences. This was not a feature that worried the

Bookers as British Guiana was so small: as recently as 1991 the population totalled only 750,000.

The abolition of slavery in 1834 caused an inward migration of indentured labour from India totalling 250,000 between 1846 and 1917. Here lay the seeds of political unrest with the indigenous population: the same thing happened in Fiji and Mauritius. The all-munificent but miserly British Colonial Office were all too aware of the problem that British rule had caused but from the 1950s onwards bequeathed emerging Guyana a Westminster-style democracy: this was swept away after independence in 1966 in the name of Marxism. Although not in power in 1966, the first President was Chedi Jagan – a US-trained Indian Guyanese dentist - and his successor Forbes Burnham nationalised everything of any size including Booker's interests in 1976, with the result that the young Republic of Guyana's economy was in permanent recession from 1970 until 1990. So sorry a state had sugar production become after nationalization in the 1970s that in 1990 Bookers, with Tate and Lyle, were contracted to manage it. Exports having fallen to 129,929 tonnes in 1990, the Booker-Tate managers worked the total up to 335,000 tonnes in 2004 with plans to take it to over 450,000 tonnes per year. The earnings began refilling the nation's empty coffers.

Booker Line

Although ships had been owned and chartered in, it was not until 1911 that the shipping operation was co-ordinated as Booker Line and the first ship, *Imataka*, built at Middlesbrough. As with many trades with a terminal port in the tropics, the ruling dimension of Booker ships down the years was a shallow draught of only 20 feet (6.0 metres) to enable them to cross the Demerara River's bar and reach the berths at Georgetown. It was from that base port that a small fleet of coasting vessels supplied Guiana's plantations and settlements, navigating the turgid rivers through humid swamps. As a commercial coincidence the long experience gained operating these coasters lead to the purchase, at head office in Liverpool, of S. William Coe and Co. Ltd. in 1955 and Metcalf Motor Coasters Ltd. in 1972.

It was not only geographic limitations of the Georgetown Bar that shaped Booker's fleet of deep sea ships but the unsophistication of back-up technical services. A wide range of talent was available back home in the South Docks in Liverpool but not over the rest of the route. This was the reason why, as late as

The *Amakura* (2) was completed at Dundee in 1924. *[B. & A. Feilden/J. & M. Clarkson]*

1949, a ship was built in which two Scotch boilers provided steam for simple reciprocating engines driving a single screw and producing a service speed of ten knots. The twelve passengers carried must have arrived in a relaxed, or alternatively frustrated, state due to inactivity and the slow-speed passages.

In the traditional ships the cargo lift was around 4,000 tonnes carried in four holds each with 'tween decks and lower holds. There was also a small amount of refrigerated cargo space. Homeward bound, bagged sugar was carried, puncheons of rum and the world's most valuable and toughest hardwood, Greenheart logs,

always the preferred material for Britain's lock gates. To obtain the maximum stow of bags in the lower holds the outer wings had unusual manhole covers up into the 'tween decks. In 1961 commercial progress ashore was to alter the shape of the fleet afloat.

From bags to bulk

By the 1960s it had become uneconomic to handle sugar in bags so Bookers were instrumental in establishing Demerara Sugar Terminals Company at Georgetown, taking the lead with a majority shareholding. Some 40,000 tonnes of bulk sugar could be stored in its £1,600,000

The *Amakura* (3) of 1949 anchored in the Mersey off the South Docks, with Cammell Laird's shipyard in the background. *[B. & A. Feilden/J. & M. Clarkson collection]*

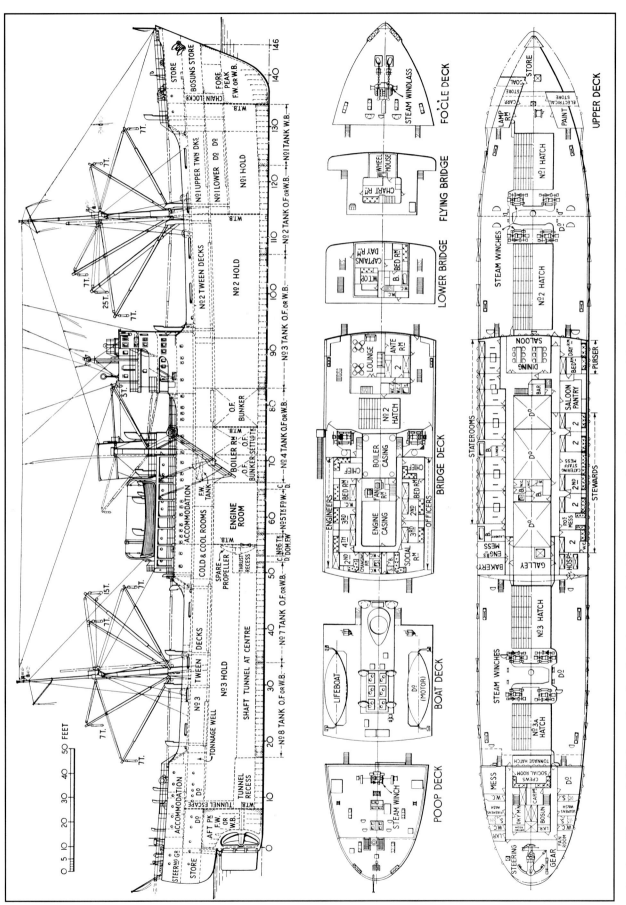

Amakura (3) was slightly larger than the *Arakaka*, completed three years earlier, had more powerful machinery and was slightly faster. There was accomodation for 12 passengers in single berth cabins, a large saloon and bar on the upper deck and a lounge and ante-room on the bridge deck. The master and officers were accommodated midships and the crew in the poop in single cabins.

The newly completed bulk carrier *Booker Venture* at anchor in the Thames. *[Peter Newall collection]*

warehouse. To export the seasonal crop Bookers ordered a new, and for them, revolutionary ship. Built to a design by Burness Corlett and Partners - at the time located in a Georgian house west of Basingstoke - *Booker Venture* was launched in February 1961 by Austin and Pickersgill at Sunderland. The builders secured the contract at a price of £900,000 and having recently spent £2,500,000 modernizing their yard a time of just 21 weeks was achieved from keel laying to sea trials. In *Booker Venture,* Burness Corlett had produced a clever design. On a hull with a beam of 62 feet (18.8 metres) and an overall length of 469 feet (143 metres), this mini bulk carrier (she had no 'tween decks) could lift 7,000 tonnes of bulk sugar on that restricted draught of 20 feet (6 metres). Three of the four large hatch covers were of the same size, 55 feet by 35 feet (16.7 by 10.6 metres). By having a double hull outboard of the holds, the grain capacity of *Booker Venture* was increased to 10,700 tonnes on a draught of 25 feet (7.6 metres). Whilst the stowage factor of bulk sugar is 43 cubic feet per tonne, that of grain is 54 cubic feet per tonne. Cleverly, Bookers now had a ship for all seasons as, when Guyana was not producing sugar, *Booker Venture* could be chartered to carry grain down the newly-opened St Lawrence Seaway.

No longer were those manning the ship accommodated in pokey, ill-ventilated centre castles. Down aft were three decks of single-berth cabins for all: in a trend-setting layout all the services were at upper deck level, including the main galley, mess rooms, laundry, hospital and ship's offices. All accommodation was air-conditioned. Gone were the 12 passenger cabins, replaced by that feature common to most cargo ships of the 1960s and 1970s, the owner's suite. An imaginative if not notably practical feature was a sweeping staircase down from the officers' lounge on the boat deck to their dining saloon alongside the swimming pool on the after end of the bridge deck. In another practice that was common at the time, the wife of Booker Line chairman Roy Rocke designed all the interior decor: photos show it reflected simple modem taste by using dominantly patterned fabrics. To Mrs Rocke and Burness Corlett goes the credit of producing a clever, habitable layout, luxurious in its day and years ahead of those of almost all other shipping companies.

Bulk carrier developments

Such was the commercial and operational success of *Booker Venture* that *Booker Vanguard* followed from

Booker Vanguard at anchor in the Mersey and dressed overall to celebrate the Queen's Silver Jubilee on 21st June 1977. *[Paul Boot]*

Burntisland in 1963 and a sister ship, *Booker Viking,* from Fredriksstad in Norway in 1967. This pair had slightly smaller hulls and, although they could carry bulk sugar in four holds, their lift on an even keel was restricted to 4,000 tonnes to get over the Georgetown bar.

What was markedly new about this pair's design was that three pairs of twin hatches covered 75% of the upper deck, so that almost all of the 296,570 cubic feet of general cargo space could be 'drop stowed' by the swinging and luffing Velle derricks plus the use of two cranes, speeding up cargo handling and reducing stevedoring costs. So querulous were Lloyd's Register about these huge hatches that, during the design stage of *Booker Vanguard*, Bumess Corlett threatened to class the ships with Det Norske Veritas who were judged more progressive in the acceptance of this feature.

The accommodation was virtually a repeat of that on *Booker Venture* right down to the sweeping staircase but there was no space for the swimming pool and the Booker Line cadets had to share a cabin. The ship's service speed of 15.5 knots was produced by a Sulzer main engine.

Above: *The Booker Vulcan* was chartered by the company in 1973 as the *Seahawk.* In 1974 she was bought outright and renamed. *[A. Denholm/Peter Newall collection]*

Above: The Swiss owned, Panamanian flag *Eugenio* was chartered in 1973 for a period of five years. Renamed *Booker Voyager* for the duration of the charter she became the *Ambri* in 1978. *[World Ship Society Limited]*

Right: The *Booker Courage*, completed in 1973 as the *Brageland* for Axel Brostrom & Son. Purchased by Bookers in 1980 she was with them for only three years before being sold to Italian buyers in 1983. *[Peter Newall collection]*

With three new ships in service and the two old steamers sold to Far Eastern buyers, Booker Line had the capacity to add other discharge ports to their southbound schedules. Before Georgetown was reached as the terminal port, the ships called at the Windward Islands and Trinidad. So well did this go with the post-independence spending spree in Commonwealth territories that the Swedish built *Johan Wessel* was time chartered and became *Booker Valiance* for ten years from 1963 until 1973. She was replaced by *Booker Vulcan*, a ship that had been built in a Polish yard in 1968. In 1979 three East German-built 'Neptune' standard type ships were purchased and renamed *Booker Challenge*, *Booker Courage* and *Booker Crusade*. They were still in service in 1984 when, to quote a historian of Bookers, 'It just seemed that the Shipping Division was by then a peripheral part of the Group which no-one wanted'. Such are the tides of history that two other shipping subsidiaries of Liverpool traders, that had so well served their parent companies, John Holt's Guinea Gulf Line and Unilever's Palm Line, were also fading away into Britain's maritime history at the same time.

Fleet list: ocean-going ships

1. IMATAKA 1911-1917

O.N. 131374 1,776g 917n
285.0 x 42.0 x 17.4 feet
T.3-cyl. Blair and Co. Ltd., Stockton-on-Tees; 320 NHP, 1,600 IHP, 12 knots.
9.1911: Completed by Sir Raylton Dixon and Co. Ltd, Middlesbrough (Yard No. 563).
5.9.1911: Registered in the ownership of Imataka Steamship Co. Ltd. (Booker Brothers, McConnell and Co. Ltd., managers), Liverpool as IMATAKA.
23.4.1917: Torpedoed and sunk by the German submarine UC 47, 15 miles south south west of Daunts Rock whilst on a

voyage from Demerara to Le Havre with a general cargo including rum, sugar and meat.
9.5.1917: Register closed.

2. AMAKURA (1) 1912-1917

O.N. 101820 2,316g 1,497n
290.6 x 38.7 x 18.5 feet
T. 3-cyl. by Robert Stephenson and Co. Ltd., Hebburn; 250 NHP, 1,100 IHP, 11 knots.
1893: Completed by C.S. Swan and Hunter, Wallsend-on-Tyne (Yard No. 170).
17.2.1893: Registered in the ownership of James Knott, Newcastle-upon-Tyne as CASTILLIAN PRINCE.

19.3.1895: Transferred to the Prince Line (1895). Ltd. (James Knott, manager), Newcastle-upon-Tyne.
6.9.1912: Sold to Samuel Cameron, Liverpool.
13.9.1912: Renamed AMAKURA
14.9.1912: Transferred to the Amakura Steam Ship Co. Ltd. (Booker Brothers, McConnell and Co. Ltd., managers), Liverpool.
12.6.1917: Torpedoed and sunk by the German submarine U 94 in the North Atlantic 180 miles north west by half west from Tory Island with a loss of two crew. She was on a voyage from Liverpool to Demerara with general cargo.
9.7.1917: Register closed.

Top: *Imataka* on trials in the Clyde.
[Glasgow University Archives DC101/ 1216(Y2)]

Right: The clipper bowed *Amakura* (1), transferred to Booker Brothers in 1912, was formerly Prince Line's *Castillian Prince.*
[World Ship Society Limited]

Grenada bought in 1913 became the first *Arakaka*. *[Glasgow University Archives DC101/0271/X1]*

3. ARAKAKA (1) 1913-1923
O.N. 105971 2,262g 1,454n
281.5 x 39.0 x 14.7 feet
T. 3-cyl. by Alexander Stephen and Sons, Glasgow; 260 NHP, 1,600 IHP, 11 knots.
1.1896: Completed by Alexander Stephen and Sons, Glasgow (Yard No. 363).
25.1.1896: Registered in the ownership of the Trinidad Shipping and Trading Co. Ltd. (George Christall, manager), Glasgow as GRENADA.
30.9.1913: Acquired by the Arakaka Steamship Co. Ltd. (Booker Brothers, McConnell and Co. Ltd., managers), Liverpool.
9.10.1913: Renamed ARAKAKA.
13.5.1924: Sold to John O. Peacock, Glasgow.
23.6.1924: Transferred to the Atlantic

Steamship Co. Ltd. (John O. Peacock, manager), Glasgow.
28.10.1924: Register closed on sale to the Hellenic Company of Maritime Enterprises (Mark P. Palios, manager), Piraeus, Greece and renamed AKI.
1928: Sold to Alex. G. Yannoulatos, Piraeus, Greece
1928: Sold to Hellenic Coast Lines Co. Ltd., Piraeus, Greece.
1938: Sold to Hellenic Mediterranean Lines, Piraeus, Greece.
11.4.1941: Sunk by air attack off Karystos in the Doro Channel whilst serving as a hospital ship.

4. AMAKURA (2) 1924-1942
O.N. 147288 1,987g 1,172n
280.1 x 42.2 x 18.7 feet

T. 3-cyl. by the Caledon Shipbuilding and Engineering Co. Ltd., Dundee; 182 NHP, 880 BHP, 1,100 IHP, 10 knots.
11.1924: Completed by the Caledon Shipbuilding and Engineering Co. Ltd., Dundee (Yard No. 293).
12.11.1924: Registered in the ownership of the Amakura Steam Ship Co. Ltd. (Booker Brothers, McConnell and Co. Ltd., managers), Liverpool as AMAKURA.
25.8.1942: Torpedoed by the German submarine U 588 100 miles off Jamaica in position 17.16 north by 52 west whilst a straggler from Convoy TAW 15 during a voyage from Liverpool via Key West to Trinidad and Demerara with general cargo and mail. Of the crew of 44, 13 were lost.
3.12.1942: Register closed.

The *Amakura* (2) docking at Liverpool. In August 1936 she was reported as being the first transatlantic steamer to arrive in Larne Harbour with mail and passengers from British Guiana for over fifty years. Also onboard was 1,500 tons of ore for the British Aluminum Company. *[B. & A. Feilden/J. & M. Clarkson]*

Arakaka (2) on trials. *[Glasgow University Archives GD320/10/1/80/2]*

5. ARAKAKA (2) 1933-1941
O.N. 162385 2,379g 1,397n
322.5 x 43.5 x 18.5 feet
12 passengers.
T.3-cyl. by David Rowan and Co. Ltd.,
Glasgow; 221 NHP, 1,160 IHP, 10 knots.
8.1933: Completed by Lithgows Ltd., Port
Glasgow (Yard No. 1157).
28.8.1933: Registered in the ownership of
the Arakaka Steamship Co. Ltd. (Booker
Brothers, McConnell and Co. Ltd.,
managers), Liverpool as ARAKAKA.
23.6.1941: Torpedoed by the German
submarine U77 in position 47 north by 40

west when acting as a weather observation
ship. All 31 crew were lost.
1.6.1942: Register closed.

6. ARAKAKA (3) 1946-1963
ON. 181020 2,814g 1,585n 4,229d
351.0 x 47.3 x 28.1. feet
T. 3-cyl by Smiths Dock Co. Ltd.,
Middlesbrough; 253 NHP, 1,700 IHP, 11
knots.
12 passengers
7.5.1946: Registered in the ownership of
the Arakaka Steam Ship Co. Ltd. (Booker
Brothers, McConnell and Co. Ltd.,

managers), Liverpool as ARAKAKA.
7.1946: Completed by Smiths Dock Co.
Ltd., Middlesbrough (Yard No. 1157).
1950: Transferred to Booker Line Ltd.
7.10.1963: Register closed on sale to
Kyriacos S. Potamianos, Athens, Greece
and renamed ABA PRINCE.
1968: Sold to Societa Industriele
Commerciale Armatoriale, Genoa, Italy and
placed under the Somali flag.
14.9.1972: Arrived at Karachi.
11.1972: Demolition began at Gadani
Beach.

Arakaka (3) in Liverpool's South Docks. *[J.K.Byass]*

7. AMAKURA (3) 1949-1961
ON. 183733 2,961g 1,588n 3,803d
335.2 x 47.3 x 18.7 feet
12 passengers.
T. 3-cyl. by Smith's Dock Co. Ltd.,
Middlesbrough; 253 NHP, 1,700 IHP, 11
knots.
6.1949: Completed by Smith's Dock Co.
Ltd., Middlesbrough (Yard No. 1180).
20.6.1949: Registered in the ownership of
the Amakura Steam Ship Co. Ltd. (Booker
Brothers, McConnell and Co. Ltd.,
managers), Liverpool as ARAKAKA.
1950: Transferred to Booker Line Ltd.
2.1.1961: Sold to Peninsula Shipping Co.
Ltd (Ocean Tramping Co. Ltd. (Chen Ja
He), managers) Hong Kong but remaining
registered at Liverpool.
13.1.1961: Renamed GREENFORD.
13.1973: Delivered to Whampoa for
demolition by the China National
Machinery Import and Export
Corporation.
30.4.1973: Register closed.

8. BOOKER VENTURE 1961-1978
O.N. 301377 8,227g 4,602n 10,700n
469.0 x 62.9 x 25.1 feet
1966: 9,516g 5,625n 12,875d
529.9 x 62.9 x 25.0 feet
Clark-Sulzer SAD 72-type 5-cyl. 2SCSA
oil engine by George Clark (Sunderland)
Ltd., Sunderland; 4,500 BHP, 14.5 knots.
14.2.1961: Launched by Austin and
Pickersgill Ltd., Sunderland (Yard No.
817).
4.1961: Completed for Booker
Merchantmen Ltd., Liverpool as
BOOKER VENTURE.

Top: *Amakura* (3) coming into Liverpool. *[J. & M. Clarkson collection]*
Middle: *Amakura* (3) at Hong Kong as the *Greenford* after her sale to buyers in the
colony. *[Roy Fenton collection]*
Lower: *Booker Venture* before lengthening in 1966. *[Captain C. L. Reynolds/Roy
Fenton collection]*

The lengthened *Booker Venture* sailing from Liverpool. *[J. & M. Clarkson]*

1961: Transferred to Booker Ship Finance Ltd. (Booker Brothers, McConnell and Co. Ltd.), London.
1962: Transferred to Booker Line Ltd., Liverpool.
1966: Lengthened.
1978: Sold to Transvenezuelan Shipping Co. S.A., Panama (Lidia Marine Corporation (M.J. Diacomanolis and G. Lirarakis), New York, USA) and renamed CARIBBEAN MEMORIES.
1980: Sold to Thanic Shipping Co. S.A., Panama (Transmar Shipping Co. S.A., Piraeus, Greece) and renamed THANIC under the Greek flag.

1985: Sold to Trader Shipping Ltd., Valletta, Malta (Stylianos Markakis, Piraeus) and renamed TRADER.
1986: Sold to Pyramis Shipping Ltd., Valletta.
10.1.1986: Breaking up began at Alang, India.

9. BOOKER VANGUARD 1963-1979
O.N. 303896 5,417g 2,522n 6,943d
403.0 x 57.0 x 30.5 feet (23. 9 feet draft)
Sulzer 6RD56-type 6-cyl. 2SCSA oil engine by Scott's Shipbuilding and Engineering Co. Ltd., Greenock; 5,000 BHP, 15.25 knots.

19.8.1963: Launched by the Burntisland Shipbuilding Co. Ltd., Burntisland (Yard No. 405).
12.1963: Completed for Booker Line Ltd., Liverpool as BOOKER VANGUARD.
1979: Sold to Ermionis Companhia Naviera S.A., Panama (Christos Kanellakis, Piraeus, Greece) and renamed KATY under the Greek flag.
1981: Sold to Chichester Shipping Corporation (Manta Line Inc., Piraeus) and renamed FRANKY.
26.11.1984: Arrived at Gadani Beach to be broken up by J.K. Brothers (PAK) Ltd.
28.11.1984: Breaking up commenced.

The *Booker Vanguard* in Scottish waters after completion by the Burntisland Shipbuilding Company Limited. *[J. Campbell Harper Ltd./Peter Newall collection]*

Booker Viking, built in Norway, was the last ship to be completed for the company. *[Peter Newall collection]*

10. BOOKER VIKING 1967-1980
O.N. 334216 5,383g 2,564n 6,800d
403.0 x 57.4 x 21.5 feet
Sulzer 6RD56-type 6-cyl. 2SCSA oil
engine by Marinens Hovedverft, Hörten,
Norway; 5,000 BHP, 15 knots.
31.3.1967: Launched by A/S Fredriksstad
Mek. Verksted, Fredriksstad (Yard No.
393).
6.1967: Completed for Booker Line Ltd.,
Liverpool as BOOKER VIKING.
1980: Sold to Qatar National Navigation
and Transport Co. Ltd., Doha, Qatar and
renamed AL AMIRAH.
19.2.1986: Breaking up began by Dewan
Sons, Gadani Beach.

11. BOOKER VOYAGER 1973-1978
4,166g 2,411n 6,082d
378.0 x 52.5 x 29.8 feet (23.5 feet draft)
Fiat 2SCSA 7-cyl. oil engine by Borsig
A.G., West Berlin; 4,000 BHP, 15 knots.
9.6.1961: Launched by Lübecker
Flenderwerke A.G., Lübeck (Yard No.
531).
1961: Completed for Hinrich Witt A.G.,
Hamburg, West Germany as HELGA
WITT.
1971: Sold to Companhia de Navigation
Puerto Nueva, Panama (World Shipping
S.A. (Sebastian Tuillier), Lugano,
Switzerland) and renamed EUGENIO.
1973: Chartered to Booker Line Ltd.,

Liverpool and renamed BOOKER
VOYAGER.
1978: Transferred to Elinkamar S.A.
Panama (World Shipping S.A. (Sebastian
Tuillier), Lugano, Switzerland) and
renamed AMBRI.
1979: Sold to Sanigul S.A. (Overland
Trust Bank), Lugano, Switzerland and
renamed GRYTTTA.
26.1.1983: Arrived Vigo, Spain.
22.8.1983: Breaking up began by Miguel
Martins Pereira.

12. BOOKER VALIANT 1978-1980
O.N. 306509 6,660g 3,527n 7,620d
429.0 x 61.0 x 25.5 feet
Burmeister & Wain-type 2SCSA 6-cyl. oil
engine by Harland and Wolff Ltd., Belfast;
7,150 BHP, 16.5 knots.
19.11.1965: Launched by the Burntisland
Shipbuilding Co. Ltd., Burntisland (Yard
No. 408).
23.4.1965: Completed for Johnston,
Warren Lines Ltd., Liverpool (Furness,
Withy and Co.Ltd, London) as NOVA
SCOTIA.
1973: Chartered to Shaw, Savill and Albion
Ltd., London and renamed TROPIC.
1974: Renamed NOVA SCOTIA.
1976: Chartered to Shaw, Savill and Albion
Ltd., London and renamed TROPIC.
1978: Acquired by Booker Line Ltd.,
Liverpool and renamed BOOKER
VALIANT.
1980: Sold to The Shipping Corporation of
Saudi Arabia Ltd., Jeddah, Saudi Arabia
and renamed ARAB DABBOR.
1986: Renamed ARAB HIND.
12.3.1998: Arrived at Alang and breaking
up began by Shri Ram Steel and Rolling.

Booker Voyager completed as the *Helga Witt* at Lubeck in 1961. *[J. & M. Clarkson]*

Booker Valiant, in the Firth of Clyde 12th February 1979. *[A. Denholm/Peter Newall collection]*

Booker Valiance. [James A. Pottinger]

13. BOOKER VALIANCE 1963-1973
4,469g 1,258n 5,950d
375.1 x 50.7 x 20.5 (29.8) feet (23.6 feet draft)
2SCSA 6-cyl. oil engine by Burmeister &
Wain Maskin-og Skibsbyggeri,
Copenhagen; 3,950 BHP, 14.5 knots.
8.3.1962: Launched by A/B Ekensberg
Varv., Stockholm, Sweden (Yard No. 227).
1962: Completed for J.H. Wessels
Kulforetning A/S & Skibs A/S Drafn
(Wessel & Norloff, managers), Drammen,
Norway as JOHAN WESSEL.
1963: Chartered to Booker Line Ltd.,
Liverpool and renamed BOOKER
VALIANCE.
6.1973: Redelivered to owners.
1973: Sold to Star Steamship Society

(Fouad and John Khayat and Co.), Beirut,
Lebanon and renamed AMIRA K.
2.5.1982: Arrived at La Spezia.
4.5.1982: Breaking up began by Cantieri
Navali Santa Maria.

14. BOOKER VULCAN 1974-1983
O.N. 358072 2,220g 1,295n 6,600d
382.2 x 35.5 x 18.8 feet
4SCSA 16-cyl oil engine by Ruston and
Hornsby Ltd., Lincoln; 4,200 BHP.
1974: Mirrlees-type 4SCSA 8-cyl. oil engine
by Mirrlees Blackstone (Stockport) Ltd.,
Stockport; 4,241 BHP, 13.5 knots made in
1973.
4.5.1968: Launched by Stocznia Gdanska im
Lenina, Gdansk (Yard No. B448/01).

8.9.1968: Completed for Sameiet Seahawk
(Graff-Wang & Evjen, managers), Oslo,
Norway as SEAHAWK.
1968: Renamed SEA VIKING.
1969: Renamed CONCORDIA SEA.
1970: Renamed SEAHAWK.
1972: Sold to They and Co. Ltd., Hamilton,
Bermuda (Ugland Management Co. A/S,
Grimstad, Norway, managers).
10.1972: Managers became Comben
Longstaff and Co. Ltd., London and Ugland
Management Co. A/S, Grimstad.
1973: Bareboat chartered to A/S Uglands
Rederi, Grimstad and registered in Singapore.
1974: Acquired by Booker Line Ltd.,
Liverpool and renamed BOOKER
VULCAN.

Booker Vulcan from the Erskine Bridge, River Clyde on 20th June 1980. *[Jim Prentice/World Ship Society Limited]*

6.1983: Sold to Star Steamship Society (Fouad and John Khayat and Co., managers), Beirut, Lebanon and renamed FOUAD K.
1984: Tranferred to Demline Egypt for Maritime Transport, Alexandria, Egypt (Fouad and John Khayat and Co., Beirut, managers) and renamed NILE CARRIER.
1995: Sold to Samatour Shipping Co. (Abdel Razzak Salem), Alexandria, Egypt and renamed SALEM TWO.
16.6.1996: Laid up at Alexandria, owners subsequently going into receivership.

2000: Sold to Charterhouse Marine Trading, Dubai.
2004: Sold to Indian breakers.

15. BOOKER CHALLENGE 1979-1983
O.N. 378097 8,336g 5,176n 11,000d
145.4 x 19.4 x 8.9 metres
MAN-type 2SCSA 6-cyl. oil engine by VEB Mascinenbau Halberstadt, Halberstadt; 9,000 BHP, 17.5 knots.
23.5.1972: Launched by VEB Schiffswerft 'Neptune', Rostock, East Germany (Yard No. 371) as SOL MICHEL.

1972: Completed for Solstads Rederi A/S (Johannes Solstad, manager), Skudeneshavn, Norway as LLOYD COPENHAGEN.
1976: Renamed SOL MICHEL.
1979: Acquired by Booker Line Ltd., Liverpool and renamed BOOKER CHALLENGE.
4.1983: Sold to Government of Nauru, Nauru (Nauru Pacific Line. Melbourne, Australia, managers) and renamed EIGUGU.

The first of the three combi-ships bought by Bookers - *the Booker Challenge* seen here in Langton Lock, Liverpool. *[Peter Newall collection]*

1990: Sold to US Trader Corporation, Monrovia, Liberia (Multifleet Marine Ltd., London, managers) and renamed US TRADER under the Bahamas flag.
1992: Sold to Evia Marine Ltd., Monrovia (G. and M. Marine Enterprises S.A., Piraeus, Greece) and renamed ELIZA under the Bahamas flag.
1994: Transferred to Deshler Incorporated, Panama (G. and M. Marine Enterprises S.A., Piraeus).
1995: Sold to Albaharia Shipping and Trading Co., Alexandria, Egypt and renamed NASR ALLAH.
1996: Sold to Summit Marine Co. Ltd., Alexandria and renamed SUMMIT.
1996: Renamed TOSHKA.
1997: Renamed SREE JI 1 under the St. Vincent flag.
3.12.1997: Arrived at Alang to be broken up by the International Steel Corporation, who began work on the same day..

16. BOOKER CRUSADE 1979-1983
O.N. 378096 8,347g 5,164n 11,000d
145.4 x 19.4 x 8.9 metres
MAN-type 2SCSA 6-cyl. oil engine by VEB Mascinenbau Halberstadt, Halberstadt; 9,000 BHP, 17.5 knots.
1975: Launched by VEB Schiffswerft 'Neptune', Rostock, East Germany (Yard No. 375).
1975: Completed for Solstads Rederi A/S (Johannes Solstad, manager), Skudeneshavn, Norway as SOL NEPTUN.
1979: Acquired by Booker Line Ltd., Liverpool and renamed BOOKER CRUSADE.
4.1983: Sold to D'Amico Societa di Navigazione S.p.A., Palermo, Italy and renamed CIELO DI TRIESTE.

Booker Crusade. [Jim Prentice/World Ship Society Limited]

1992: Transferred to Alhambra Shipping Ltd., Monrovia, Liberia (D'Amico Societa di Navigazione S.p.A., Rome, Italy).
1993: Sold to Jutha Maritime plc, Bangkok, Thailand and renamed JUTHA PHANSIRI.
1998: Sold to Majestic Maritime Ltd., Valletta, Malta (International Maritime and Marine Services (London) Ltd., Croydon) and renamed MAJESTIC K.
1998: Transferred to Queen Haja Navigation Inc., Panama (IM Marine Services (London) Ltd., London) (Metkar Shipping and Trading Co. S.r.L., Constanta, Roumana, managers) and renamed QUEEN HAJA.
3.2006: Still listed by Lloyd's Register.

17. BOOKER COURAGE 1980-1983
O.N. 389160 8,522g 4,773n 11,045d
145.5 x 19.4 x 8.9 metres
MAN-type 2SCSA 6-cyl. oil engine by VEB Mascinenbau Halberstadt, Halberstadt; 9,000 BHP, 17.5 knots.

11.5.1973: Launched by VEB Schiffswerft 'Neptune', Rostock, East Germany (Yard No. 373).
1973: Completed for A/B Svenska Orient Linien (Axel Brostrom & Son), Gothenburg, Sweden as BRAGELAND.
1980: Acquired by Booker Line Ltd., Liverpool and renamed BOOKER COURAGE.
4.1983: Sold to D'Amico Societa di Navigazione S.p.A., Palermo, Italy and renamed CIELO DI LIVORNO.
1988: Sold to World Trader Corporation, Monrovia, Liberia (Multifleet Marine Ltd., London, managers) and renamed WORLD TRADER under the Bahamas flag.
1991: Sold to Jiangsu Marine Shipping Co., Nanjing, People's Republic of China and renamed SU YU.
1993: Transferred to Jiangsu Nantong Shipping School, Nanjing.
3.2006: Still listed by Lloyd's Register.

Booker Courage, the third combi-carrier, in the Crosby Channel, River Mersey on 19th May 1982. Although the three ships had been very successful, in July 1982 it was announced that with the Guyana trade running at only 10% of its volume of a year before the company had no alternative but to lay up the three ships as they returned to Liverpool. They were replaced with smaller chartered ships the first of which was the German *Krusau* (4,972/1978) which left Liverpool at the end of July. *[Paul Boot]*

SAILING TANKERS
Part 2: true bulk carriers
John Naylon

From the mid-1880s onwards there was a rapid growth in trans-Atlantic oil traffic. Since the late 1870s the Pennsylvania Transportation Company's pipeline to the US east coast had gradually increased the flow of oil and was stimulating the construction of new large coastal refineries, tank farms, and pumping and bulk-handling facilities. Perhaps more importantly, Standard Oil (incorporated in 1870 with John D. Rockefeller as president) had come to account for 30 per cent of US oil production, over 75 per cent of refining capacity, and over 90 per cent of pipelines – exerting effective control over the total international supply of US oil. By deliberately restricting supplies to the US domestic market (in order to maintain prices) substantial surpluses were made available for export. From 0.8 million barrels in 1880 US exports rose to 1.5 million in 1885 and 14.7 million in 1889. With shipments across the Atlantic reaching 2.3 million tons in 1900, parcel shipments in cases or barrels were unable to cope (falling to only one per cent of the Atlantic tonnage) and a demand was created for purpose-built bulk carriers.

There were initial technical and commercial concerns to overcome. Ship owners feared the effects of oil on metal hulls (weakening rivets; cargo movements causing stresses in high seas) and the need to amortize quickly the costs of construction and return ballast passages. Classification societies such as Lloyd's Register and Bureau Veritas and insurance companies worried about the risks of fire and explosion. Resistance was gradually overcome by improved construction techniques – better riveting methods; reinforcement of hulls to resist surging; systems to allow for the expansion and contraction of the oil – which allowed the appearance of a new generation of nine iron and steel square riggers using the hull itself as container. These metal-hulled sailing vessels were stronger, easier to load and unload, had greater carrying capacity, and were better insurance risks against fire and stranding, permitting the discarding of the wasteful double-containment system.

Hainaut

In 1887 the Barrow Shipbuilding Company (later to become the Naval Construction and Armaments Company and finally Vickers-Armstrong Ltd.)

launched the first of this new generation of sailing tankers – the steel full-rigger *Hainaut* (named after a Belgian province) – for F. Speth & Co. of Antwerp. Of 1,783gt and 1,659nt on dimensions 248.8 x 40.3 x 22.2 feet, she was able to carry 2,525 tons of petroleum in her ten tanks. The *Hainaut* had a smart turn of speed, making as many as four passages a year between New York and Antwerp. In 1891 she was acquired by the American Petroleum Company of Rotterdam, in 1910 by Anglo-American, and in 1912 by the Tank Storage and Carriage Co. Ltd. of London – all in the process of Standard Oil's reorganization after falling foul of the United States' anti-trust laws. In 1914 she went to the Compañía Cubana de Transportes de Mieles of Havana, was renamed *Martí*, and in 1950 was still afloat as a molasses barge.

Ville de Dieppe

From the outset France was a big importer of US oil – usually crude, since up to 1903 heavy import tariffs were levied on refined products in order to stimulate domestic refining. The first 'modern' French sailing tanker, the *Ville de Dieppe*, was launched in 1888 at Southampton by the prolific sailing-ship builders Oswald, Mordaunt and Co. for L. Robbe et Fils of Dieppe. A steel and iron barque of 1,254gt and 1,228nt on dimensions 217.0 x 36.4 x 21.0 feet, she had a capacity of 1,200 tons of oil in six tanks, isolated fore and aft by water-filled cofferdams. In 1900, after being badly damaged by fire, she was sold to Prentout-Leblond of Rouen (of whom more anon)

Dieppe
Le Trois-Mâts " Ville-de-Dieppe "
et le Port de demi-marée

The *Ville de Dieppe* was the last vessel (Yard No.253) built by Oswald, Mordaunt at their Woolston yard, Southampton, before the company went into liquidation and relocated to Milford Haven. *[Jürgen Meyer collection]*

and then in July 1903 passed into the hands of Akties. Union (Jens Pay, manager) of Christiania, Norway, retaining her original name. After a successful career of 29 years, mainly trading between Philadelphia and the Dieppe refinery, she fell a neutral victim to Germany's unrestricted submarine warfare, being sunk by gunfire by UC 21 in April 1917, 21 miles west of the Isle of Oléron, on passage from La Pallice to New York in ballast.

Calcutta ex-*Unionen*

In 1892 the Barrow yard – by now the Naval Construction and Armaments Company – launched a virtual sister ship (apart from her rig) to the *Hainaut*: the steel three-masted barque *Unionen*, built for the Vestlandske Petroleums Kompagni of Bergen, Norway (who would later acquire the *Rendova*; see below). Of 1,694gt and 1,578nt on dimensions 248.8 x 40.2 x 21.9 feet, she had a load displacement of 3,570 tons on an 18.2 foot draught, with 2,540 tons of oil, crew and stores, and carried 23,155 square feet of canvas. Like the *Hainaut*, the *Unionen*'s hold was divided into ten tanks by a centreline bulkhead and six transverse bulkheads, leaving the 'tween decks available for dry cargo. As was usual in this type of vessel, the masts were stepped not on the keelson but on the 'tween decks. Petroleum could be unloaded in 24 hours by the ships' own pumps, worked by a large donkey boiler which also drove the winches and – in the case of the *Unionen* – a dynamo which provided electric light in the accommodation (but not for the navigation lights, being considered too unreliable). The crews were berthed in the actual topgallant forecastles.

After passing briefly through the hands of the Channel Drydock Shipbuilding and Engineering Company of Passage West, Cork, Ireland, in 1901 the *Unionen* was acquired by Anglo-American and renamed *Calcutta*. In 1912, like the *Hainaut*, she was transferred to the Tank Storage and Carriage Company, only to return to Anglo-American in 1915.

Captain J. Williamson, who served in the *Calcutta*, described her as 'a brute to steer' with her very flat bottom and full ends (*Sea Breezes*, Old Series, Vol.18, 1934, pp.245-7). Although built with bilge keels, these did not seem to prevent the *Calcutta*'s rolling antics and, like the *Hainaut*, she made a habit of dismasting herself. In December 1904, on passage from Leith to Philadelphia in ballast, while head reaching in heavy weather, she brought down her fore and main topgallant masts, threw the helmsman over the wheelbox and smashed the wheel. In 1908 she lost her topmasts in a typhoon off Japan, and again the next year in the North Pacific. Nevertheless, Captain Williamson, who also served in Anglo-American's four-masted barque *Daylight*, describes both vessels as 'well equipped with gear and good living ships for that period'.

For the first six years of her career with Anglo-American the *Calcutta*'s regular routine was to load oil at Point Breeze, Philadelphia, for Calcutta and return with sugar, rice and sago to Europe or the United States, each round

The *Calcutta* ex-*Unionen*, here seen at anchor off San Francisco, was unusual among British-built sailing vessels in having German-style double gaffs on the mizzen. The big coal-fired donkey boilers of the *Calcutta* and *Hainaut* also drove the cargo pumps and had tall stacks to obtain the necessary draught. [*San Francisco Maritime National Historical Park B6. 3,650*]

voyage taking about a year. From 1906 to 1915 she was diverted to the Pacific, trading from San Francisco to Shanghai and Yokohama – making a very fast voyage in 1907 of 47 days from San Francisco to Shanghai and returning in 34 days after only five days in port. Returning to home waters in 1915 she became a fuelling depot for destroyers at Falmouth.

After the First World War the *Calcutta*, by now the last unit of the great Anglo-American sailing fleet, was refitted to carry cadets and put back into the trans-Atlantic oil trade; but this programme soon collapsed. She made her last bulk oil passage in 1921, leaving New York on 21st July and arriving at Avonmouth on 14th August. Withdrawn and moored in Southampton Water opposite Hamble, to serve as a fuel barge, she went to the Dutch shipbreakers T.G. Pas of Scheveningen in 1923 after 30 years of service.

Alice et Isabelle

In France the *Ville de Dieppe* was followed in 1893 by the steel three-masted barque *Alice et Isabelle*, managed by Prentout-Leblond although actually owned by P. Lesourd et Fils and the Gramont Refinery Society. The first vessel of her type built in France, she ran over her estimated cost so much that the Compagnie Générale Transatlantique's Penhoët shipyard at Saint Nazaire did not tender for any subsequent sailing tankers. She was a small, fine-lined vessel for her time: 731gt, carrying only a similar tonnage of oil in four tanks in the lower hold (plus water-filled tanks forward and aft as cofferdams) and with room for 800 barrels in the 'tween decks. To maintain stability her tanks could only be emptied one at a time, the empty tank being immediately filled with sea water; similarly, her return passages across the Atlantic were made with the tanks filled with sea water; and the fear of fire was still such that the *Alice et Isabelle*'s pump for discharging could only be operated by a steam engine ashore. Despite this precaution she caught fire twice. With a crew of only twelve,

she traded between Marcus Hook (Philadelphia) and Sables d'Olonne (her home port), supplying the west of France in the same way as the *Ville de Dieppe* served the north. In 1909, after 16 years under the French flag, she was bought by the Norwegian company Valla Oilizafinaderi, a subsidiary of the Danish Petroleum Society of Copenhagen, and renamed *Dieselea* (and in 1912 *Astrid*). At the end of the First World War she was back in the hands of the Danske Petroleums Akties. (C. From Holm, Copenhagen, manager) but they disposed of her in 1923 and she disappears from the register.

Quévilly

In contrast to the modest size of her predecessor, the steel four-masted barque *Quévilly* of 1897 – probably the best-known and most handsome of all the tank sailers – measured 3,482gt on dimensions 322.0 x 45.5 x 24.2 feet and reflected the enthusiasm for bulk oil transport of her owner Henri Prentout-Leblond of Rouen. In association with E. Boniface and later E. Leroux, Prentout-Leblond was a very substantial owner and manager of sailing ships and holds a special place in French maritime history: in 1911 he became the owner of the largest sailing vessel ever built, the 5,633gt five-masted barque *France* (2).

The *Quévilly* would most likely have been called *Ville de Rouen* had not Prentout-Leblond already owned a vessel of that name. Called after the *faubourg* of Rouen where she was built by Laporte et Compagnie (Chantiers de Normandie), she took to the water at 3.30 p.m. on 20th March 1897 and was blessed by Monsignor Sourrieu, Archbishop of Rouen, before a crowd of 6,000. Built on the same lines as Bordes' *Dunquerque*, which preceded her down the ways, the new tanker was completed in June.

Her three-island hull responded to the *prime* paid by the French government under the law of 1893 (renewed in 1902), whereby a bounty of 65 francs per gross ton was paid to owners of steel vessels, in practice favouring the building of ships of around 3,000 tons and giving rise to the extensive superstructures of latter-day French deepwatermen. Thus, the *Quévilly* measured only 1,701 net tons as against her gross tonnage of 3,482, thanks to an 88-foot forecastle, a 32-foot midships bridge and a 104-foot poop – structures which constituted the actual working deck and gave her the reputation of a good sea boat, taking little water on board. Carrying over 48,000 square feet of canvas, her fore, main and mizzen masts rose 173 feet above the deck and bore 93-foot lower yards and 50-foot royals. She could load 3,750 tons of oil in twelve tanks, divided by a longitudinal bulkhead, in the lower hold, plus case oil in the 'tween decks. She could be loaded by gravity in American ports (e.g., Marcus Hook, Philadelphia) in 30 hours and discharged by pumps in 48 hours

Entrée de l' « Alice-et-Isabelle » dans le Port des SABLES-D'OLONNE

Nouvelle Collection Vendéenne, Lucien Amiaud, Sables d'Olonne, N: 2

The *Alice et Isabelle* running into her home port of Sables d Olonne. A wet ship, known to her crews as the submarine , she made a fast passage from Marcus Hook in 13 days. In the absence of a tug, entering and leaving Sables d Olonne was often effected *à la cordelle* — men, women and children hauling the vessel along the jetty *[Lucien Amiaud/Jürgen Meyer collection]*

in France (e.g., at Grand Quévilly, Rouen). On her outward ballast passages she carried 2,800 tons of sea water. Two coal-fired boilers worked two pumps which could discharge 100 tons an hour as well as providing heating, fresh water and power for the winches. A petrol generator provided electric light. Registered in Le Havre, she bore the signal letters KSFM and carried a crew of 32-36 all told.

The *Quévilly* was a steady and successful earner, mostly on a regular route between Marcus Hook or Bayonne and Rouen or Dieppe, but also loading in Texas and New York and discharging in Calais, Dunkirk, Rotterdam, La Pallice and Sète. Despite not being over-sparred and having rather full ends she was a powerful ship, capable of making

613. *Dieppe.* — L'Avant-Port

The *Quévilly* manoeuvring in the outer harbour of Dieppe. Her arrival at this small port always attracted a crowd of spectators. *[G. Marchand/Author's collection]*

good runs and touching 15.5 knots in strong winds. During her first two years of operation her average westward passage was 36 days and average eastward passage 26 days, with an average duration per round voyage of 63 days, including stays in port. However, she could do substantially better than this. In November 1898 she ran from the Delaware breakwater to Le Havre in 17 days, beating the steamer *Mexican Prince* which had set out at the same time but took 18 days; and in 1906 she made the same passage in 14 days, leaving the Delaware six hours after the steam tanker *Oilfield* and arriving at Le Havre only four hours behind. Her fastest westward crossing was from Le Havre to the Delaware breakwater in 19 days, and her fastest eastward crossing was twelve and a half days. On the other hand – illustrating the vagaries of sail – she once took 103 days from Le Havre to Bayonne; even so, she arrived at the same time as the barque *Amiral de Cornulier* which had set out two weeks earlier and had been given up for lost. The *Quévilly* received bonuses if a round trip was made in 50 days or less and if she made five voyages in the year; the crew also received an extra month's pay. She even carried carrier pigeons to report progress. Needless to say, this was a punishing regime, involving only two or three days' turn-round and causing heavy wear and tear on sails and gear. To expedite matters she was always towed from Rouen or Dieppe to the Lizard. Altogether, the *Quévilly* made 84 round voyages across the Atlantic, usually by the northern route in summer and the southern route in winter.

Although successful as a pure sailing ship, in order further to sharpen her schedule the *Quévilly* was fitted in 1911 with two modestly-powered diesel engines of the type then used in submarines. Driving twin screws, the single-acting, two-stroke, six-cylinder motors of 96 nominal horse power were installed by the Maschinenfabrik Augsburg-Nürnberg A.G. (M.A.N.) and the experiment was closely watched by other sailing-ship owners who were considering fitting auxiliary engines. In the event (and as other experiments proved) the engines were of doubtful value. Although they were trouble-

free; although they saved on towage in the English Channel and on entering some ports; and although fuel could be bought cheaply in Philadelphia or New York, they were not as economically justifiable as expected. The engines were expensive and slow to pay for themselves. Against the five or six knots which they provided in the rare calms of the North Atlantic, the *Quévilly* lost at least two knots throughout her voyages because of the drag of the propellers. They did not shorten her round voyages, which remained at 49-65 days. There was a loss of cargo space. The ship was still unable to dispense completely with tugs because the motors were unable to overcome the windage of the top hamper. The engineer had to be added to the pay roll, at a wage nearly four times that of a sailor; in order to justify his pay he had to play the roles of carpenter and blacksmith as well.

The *Quévilly* continued on her regular but now highly-dangerous run for most of the First World War, her only mishap occurring on 26th January 1917 when she was rammed by the US destroyer *Samson* while entering New York in fog (although the *Samson* was judged to be at fault the $8,400 damages were not paid by the United States government until 1934). By late 1917, however, her speed under power was considered insufficient to evade German submarines lurking in the Western Approaches, whose chosen prey were sailing vessels, and early in the following year she was sent to St. Michael's in the Azores as an oil-storage and bunkering ship (while *en route* she narrowly missed being torpedoed off La Pallice on 11th February 1918). She resumed trade between Philadelphia and France in March 1919 but her glory days were over. In December 1920 she went aground off Dunkirk when her anchor chain parted; although she came off undamaged it was evident that she could no longer compete with modern powered tankers, especially given the post-war slump in freight rates, and on 5th October 1921 she was laid up at Croisset (Rouen). Moreover, in 1920 the eight-hour working day had been introduced into the French merchant marine, giving rise to larger crews and increased costs of overtime

Quévilly as the Norwegian *Deodata* after conversion to a motor ship. *[J. & M. Clarkson collection]*

(the *Quévilly*'s crew increased in number from 36 to 45 men); and in 1921 the *prime* system lapsed. It is also worth recalling that when the giant *France* (2) went aground in 1922 near Noumea, New Caledonia, it was not considered worthwhile even to attempt salvage and her hull was sold for £2,000.

In April 1923 the *Quévilly* was sold by her owners (by now Leroux et Heuzey of Rouen) to A/S Sörlandske Lloyd (K.A. Thorbjornsen, manager) of Oslo, Norway, who converted her into a full-powered motor ship. Her masts and spars were removed, leaving her with two pole masts; two new six-cylinder, four-stroke, single-acting diesel engines of 209 nominal horsepower were installed by A/S Holeby Dieselmotor Fabrik; and she was given a new superstructure and funnel right aft. She left Rouen on 13th March 1924 for Port Arthur, Texas, in her new role as a mineral oil and whale oil carrier.

Renamed *Deodata* in 1926, the old ship's ownership changed several times. In 1928 she was bought by Skibs A/S Deodata of Horten, Norway (Chr. Hannevig, Asgardstrand, manager) and was latterly employed carrying Black Sea oil to French, British and Baltic ports. She was an early casualty of the Second World War. On 21st October 1939, bound from Constanza, Romania, to Grangemouth in ballast, she struck a mine which had been laid five days earlier by U 19 (Kapitan-Leutnant Hans Meckel) one and a half miles off the Inner Dowsing light vessel. The crew of 23 were rescued, although three were badly injured.

France-Marie and Jules Henry

The final French contributions were the sister ships *France-Marie* and *Jules Henry*, launched on 17th January and 19th March 1900, respectively, by Forges et Chantiers de la Méditerranée at Graville, Le Havre, for Adolphe Vimont et Cie., Marseille. The Vimont firm had been set up two years earlier and owned just the two vessels: steel barques of 2,088gt and 1,066nt on dimensions 250.0 x 40.2 x 23.5 feet. Their ten tanks, carrying 2,400 tons of oil, were divided by a longitudinal bulkhead, with water-filled cofferdams fore and aft. Steam boilers provided power for electricity, winches and pumps which could discharge 100 tons per hour, emptying the vessel in 30 hours. Both ships were in the Philadelphia to Marseille trade, although the *France-Marie* made occasional deliveries at such Spanish ports as Santander, Vigo, Alicante, Valencia, Tarragona and Palma de Mallorca. Unusually, Vimont advertised his vessels as carrying British-style apprentices (*pilotins*), not normal French practice.

The *France-Marie* made 55 round voyages Philadelphia to Marseille for Vimont between 1900 and 1908. The average duration of her west-bound passages from

Gibraltar to Philadelphia was 35.6 days (longest passage 46 days; shortest 24 days, twice) and of her east-bound passages Philadelphia to Gibraltar 23.9 days (longest 40 days; shortest 17 days, twice). Her experience illustrates the unreliability of winds in the Mediterranean and the difficulty of clearing the Straits of Gibraltar: in 1900 she took 34 days to go from Marseille to Gibraltar, while making Marseille from Gibraltar in only five days on four other occasions. The *France-Marie* was sold in 1911 to the Continental Petroleum Company of Belgium and in 1912 was transferred to the Texas Company of Port Arthur, U.S.A., who converted her into a three-masted schooner barge and renamed her *Tampico*. In 1943 she was still in use as a floating wharf at New Orleans.

The *France-Marie* in the *Vieux Port* of Marseille. *[Jürgen Meyer collection]*

The *Jules Henry* made a record passage in March 1901 of 19 days 12 hours from Marcus Hook, Philadelphia, to Marseille under Captain Beaudouart, but she is best remembered for her explosion in 1909 in the Pinède Basin at Marseille. At 9.45 a.m. on 1st April, the ship having arrived a few days before from Philadelphia and discharged, the first mate went into the forward tank with an electric lamp which probably short-circuited. The resulting blast ripped up 100 feet of the deck and hurled the masts over the starboard rail. Nine men were killed and 13 more seriously injured.

The barque was repaired at great expense but in 1913 was sent by Vimont to be converted into a full-powered motorship by Wilton's Engineering & Slipway Company, Rotterdam. The hull was cut in two amidships and lengthened by 50.8 feet, increasing the oil tank capacity to 2,800 tons and the gross tonnage to 2,505. Seven divided tanks could now carry three different kinds of oil and two 12-cylinder engines of 675 ihp were installed by Werkspoor of Amsterdam, to give a speed of eight knots. The last bulk sailing tanker built in France thus became the country's first motor ship. Vimont (now styling himself the Compagnie Française de Navires-Citernes) put the *Jules Henry* into the Black Sea trade between Constanza and Marseille, with a martial interlude providing drinking water for the troops in the Dardanelles. After being laid up at Le Havre in 1933 she was broken up at Hamburg the following year.

The long poop and forecastle head of the *Jules Henry* denote a 'bounty ship'. Like some other latter-day French sailing ships, she and the *France-Marie* carried stockless anchors. [Musée National de la Marine, Paris PH 85774]

Sunlight and *Rendova*

The last two sailing tankers to be built as such were also the last two square riggers built in Great Britain for British owners. Bald-headed three-masted steel barques of 1,432gt, the *Sunlight* and *Rendova* were launched in 1907 by Napier and Miller Ltd. of Old Kilpatrick, Dunbartonshire, for Lever Brothers, the soap manufacturers of Port Sunlight, Cheshire. Something of their character and careers has been described in an earlier issue of this journal ('The last square riggers built for British owners', Record 29, November 2004, pp.34-6).

According to *Lloyd's Weekly Shipping Index* their hulls were divided by nine bulkheads. A fore-and-aft bulkhead in the oil space formed ten tanks, in addition to which, besides the peak tanks, general cargo could be carried in the 'tween decks and in a fore hold. They were well equipped with machinery: a large boiler serving a donkey pump and a steam winch for working general cargo; two powerful duplex double-acting pumps for handling oil cargoes; and a fresh-water condensing plant. However, their sea-going abilities left something to be desired: they were said to be heavy to manoeuvre, would not run, and continually broached-to in heavy weather.

They were originally intended to bring palm oil from Rendova Island in the Pacific to Port Sunlight. In practice, they made only brief appearances 'Down Under'. Both took general cargoes out to Sydney on their maiden voyages and returned with palm oil to Liverpool, and the *Rendova* repeated this voyage in 1910. For the rest of their short careers they settled into the more rewarding oil trade from Philadelphia, Port Arthur and New York, and the molasses trade from Macoris, Haiti, and were so engaged when they were lost to submarine attack in the Irish Sea approaches during the First World War. The *Sunlight*, which had been under charter to the United Molasses Co. Ltd. since 1910, was torpedoed on 6th June 1915 20 miles south west of Galley Head, on passage Macoris to Glasgow with bulk molasses and bagged sugar. The *Rendova* (since 1915 under the Norwegian flag as the *Snespurven*, owned by the Vestlandske Petroleums Co. of Bergen) was sunk by gunfire on 2nd April 1917 in the St George's Channel, on passage New York-Dublin with petroleum.

The *Sunlight* alongside the oil storage tank at Sydney during her maiden voyage in 1907. [State Library of South Australia, Edwardes collection]

[To be concluded in Record *35]*

THE SOUTHDOWN STEAMSHIP CO. LTD.
David Burrell

Georgia, bought from her builders, William Gray and Co., Sunderland in 1894 by S.V. Symondson. *[Nigel Farrell collection]*

Stanley Vernon Symondson (c 1862-1906) is first recorded as a member of the Baltic Exchange in 1886. He commenced ship management in London in 1892 with the eight-year-old steamer *John Stevenson* (named for a Whitby author, 1718-1785), bought from Thomas Smailes and Son of Whitby and renamed *Vernon.* As a Lloyd's underwriter Symondson would have been deeply involved in marine insurance. The freight market had been badly depressed through the 1880s with few, minor, recoveries to steady a downward trend. The failure, and reconstruction, of Baring Brothers in November 1890 intensified the depression, which continued into the mid-1890s. Symondson may well have felt the time was ripe for a period of prosperity in shipping, as many identified a ten-year cycle in the shipping market.

A year later the similar *Invermay* was acquired from Thomas Turnbull and Sons, Whitby whose Whitehall shipyard had built both her and *Vernon.* In January 1894 *Vernon* was wrecked in the Baltic, and the slightly larger Gray-built *Georgia* bought from her builders. *Invermay* was sold to Italian buyers in 1896.

The family had been engaged in the Lloyd's insurance market since at least 1839. The 1881 census records Stanley and brother Herbert as underwriting clerks, whilst their uncle, William Symondson (born 1837), was shown as an insurance broker in returns to the Registrar of Companies. Both Stanley

and Herbert joined William Symondson and Co. and received their business training from William. Insurance remained their main business as underwriting members of Lloyd's, but like others at Lloyd's (e.g. Bolton and Lamplough) they diversified into ship owning.

With only *Georgia* left Symondson formed a partnership with Thomas Bell of Newcastle-upon-Tyne as Bell, Symondson and Co. to manage the Southdown Steamship Co. Ltd. which was incorporated in August 1897. Both men were directors of Southdown, as was William Symondson. *Georgia* was transferred to the company on 2nd December 1897 for £10,240, each 64th shareholder (Symondson had 17) receiving £20 cash and fourteen £10 shares. This brought an association with Pymans, although financial control lay with Bell. Southdown's flag bore no resemblance to the Pyman flags, but a family likeness can be discerned in the funnel colours. Both were black, on which Pyman placed a black ball on a broad white band. Southdown had a white ball between two narrow white bands.

Thomas Bell (1841-1914) was a partner in Pyman, Bell and Co. of Newcastle-upon-Tyne. George Pyman (1822-1900) was a shipmaster from Whitby who settled in West Hartlepool in the early 1850s and turned to steam. Pyman companies and offices were to be found from Glasgow to Cardiff, London and Hull as well as in Sweden and Finland. In addition to ship

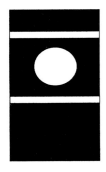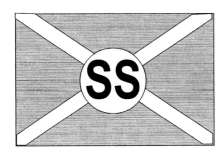

Flag and funnel of the Southdown Steamship Co. Ltd. The flag had a blue ground. *[J.L. Loughran]*

owning, Pyman's interests included coal and timber. Thomas Bell was sent to open a Newcastle branch of George Pyman and Co. in 1864, being taken into partnership in 1873 with the company becoming Pyman, Bell and Co. He was Mayor of Newcastle-upon-Tyne in 1889-1890.

The authorised capital of Southdown was £50,000, raised to £100,000 in 1899 and £150,000 in 1906. Only 10,000 £10 shares were ever issued, and these were only partly paid up, the paid-up figure reaching £72,688 in 1905 and thereafter remaining at that level. Loans and mortgages financed the fleet; the five ships owned in 1914 had cost £166,537 to build. They operated as tramps, typically loading coal out to the Mediterranean, returning from the Black Sea with grain, and also participating in the developing River Plate trade.

A 3,600 deadweight steamer had been ordered from Osbourne, Graham and Co. of Sunderland at a cost of £23,152, and was named *Rustington* when launched on 27th August 1897 by a daughter of Alderman Bell. She had a bad year in 1901, grounding three times: 16th January in the Plate, 6th June in the Bristol Channel and 9th October in the River Paraguay.

Nomenclature matched the company name; parishes and manors on the Sussex Downs. The slightly larger

Novington followed in May 1899, from Richardson, Duck and Co., Stockton-on-Tees who were to build all the fleet until 1912. She cost £29,106. A sister followed in August 1900, launched by Mrs Ernest Bell and named *Dallington*. The buoyant freight market during the Boer War was reflected in her price of £33,450. The outbreak of the Spanish-American War in 1898, followed by the Boer War in October 1899 and the Boxer Rising in China (1900) soon resulted in a shortage of tonnage for charter, and the Southdown accounts quickly reflected this. Prior to the First World War, the Boer War was the largest military expedition ever undertaken by the British Government, who chartered some two million tons of shipping as troop transports and supply ships both to support the troops committed to the conflicts and to abate plague and famine in India.

Whereas the three second hand ships were raised quarterdeck 'tween deckers, those built in and after 1897 were single deckers. Initially they were three island ships, but beginning with *Levington* in 1905 the bridge deck was doubled in length and thereafter only long bridge deckers were built. *Rustington* (3) of 1924 had a 225-foot bridge deck on a length of 360 feet.

Georgia was sold in 1902. To replace her a contract was signed in January 1903 for a slightly larger vessel costing £29,808. Launched on 9th July by Mrs Stanley Symondson as *Lullington* she made her first voyage to the Sea of Azov. The builders received £30,639 for the next addition, *Jevington*, completed in July 1905. The following year the *Rustington* of 1897 was sold to Cardiff owners.

In September 1906 Stanley Symondson died, leaving an estate of £53,320 (the equivalent of over £2 million today). His seat as a director was taken by Thomas Bell's son Thomas Herbert Bell (1870-1933), reflecting the Bell financial interest in Southdown. In December 1897 of 3,425 shares issued, the Bell family held 1,060, Symondsons 964 and Pymans 53. By 1917 of the 10,000 issued the spread was 4,480, 843 and 180 respectively.

Dallington, completed in August 1900 lasted until 1933 when she was broken up in Italy. *[George Scott collection]*

Rustington (2) lasted for only eight years. Completed in 1909 she was torpedoed and sunk in 1917. *[Nigel Farrell collection]*

Financial policy was conservative; dividends for 1901 to 1911 ranging from 5% to 7%. This was a period of recession and many companies failed to pay dividends. Southdown kept their profit and loss account in the black, profits ranging from £8,504 to £18,913. At the same time regular transfers were made for depreciation, totalling £54,858. With the fleet valued at £104,220 this closely matched new costs. Depreciation was increased in the early war years, and by 1916 the ships had been written down to £62,397.

The sale of *Rustington* (1) in 1906 was balanced by commissioning *Rustington* (2) in 1909. A similar change followed in 1911 when *Novington* went to Swedish buyers. Her replacement, *Novington* (2), was launched in May 1912. The same year Stanley Symondson's older brother Herbert Walter Symondson (1858-1928) replaced as a director William Symondson, who had retired the previous year.

On the outbreak of war in September 1914 the fleet stood at five, three of which would be war losses, fortunately without loss of life. *Lullington* had arrived at Antwerp from Rosario and *Dallington* was at Matanzas. *Jevington* was at San Nicolas loading for the UK and *Rustington* (2) on passage from Gulfport for Buenos Aires, whilst *Novington* (2) had arrived at New York from Rosario. Thomas Bell died in September 1914, his seat on the board being taken by his son Frederick Bell (1873-1937).

It was to be 1915 before any Southdown ships were requisitioned. In February 1915 *Lullington* was taken as Collier 536, followed by *Rustington* (2) in May as Collier 635. Apart from two months in 1916, *Lullington* was to remain on Government service until lost in February 1917. Similarly *Rustington* (2) had few months off requisition before being sunk in April 1917. *Jevington* was the only ship not requisitioned. January 1916

saw both *Dallington* and *Novington* (2) taken up, as Colliers 995 and 152; *Dallington* not being released until the end of March 1919. *Novington* (2) saw similar service, latterly as Expeditionary Force transport D1206 until released in March 1919.

Full employment, with some ships left on the open charter market, had a marked impact on the accounts. It has been estimated that the index figure for charter rates during and after the First World War, with the period 1890 to 1899 = 100, were:

1915	323	1918	2,492
1916	634	1919	561
1917	1,841	1920	330

Jevington was the first war loss, sunk on 23rd January 1917. The next month, *Lullington* whilst running as an Admiralty collier, hit a mine laid off Hastings. On 25th July, *Rustington* (2) was hit by U 54. *Novington* (2) had three brushes with the enemy. A torpedo missed in the Mediterranean in February 1917, and in August one hit but failed to explode off the Shetlands. But on 24th October 1917, with sawn wood from Archangel for Nantes, she was hit and damaged by UC 40 whilst in convoy 25 miles east of the Shetlands. Beached in Cullingsburgh Bay, Bressay, she was later refloated and repaired. *Dallington* was missed twice in the English Channel, in October 1917 and August 1918. The Government made war loss payments through Southdown's P&I Club, the United Kingdom Mutual War Risks Association, (see below) although no explanation is known for the disparity between the sums paid.

In 1918 the Shipping Controller placed two ships under Bell, Symondson management, the B-class *War Parrot* and *War Pigeon*. Both were sold in 1919, but three former German ships were entrusted to management that year.

War loss insurance payments made through the UK P&I Club					
Name	**Loss date**	**Year/gt**	**Cost new**	**Loss paid**	**Cargo**
Jevington	23.1.1917	1905/2,747	£30,639	£ 30,000	Wheat
Lullington	8.2.1917	1903/2,816	£29,808	£124,256	Coal
Rustington (2)	25.7.1917	1909/3,071	?	£ 39,250	Iron ore

The third *Rustington*, the company's last ship. *[George Scott collection]*

November 1918 found *Dallington* and *Novington* (2) at sea. They had been written down to £6,500 and £15,397 in the accounts which, with war insurance payments and steady employment, revealed investments of £386,334. These enabled Southdown to survive the 1920s, when many companies without this cushion failed. Not being over capitalised, Southdown paid dividends of 30% in 1922-24, followed by 17.5 % in 1925-6 and 25% in 1927, 22.5 % in 1928, 20 % in 1929 and 10% in 1930. In 1925 and 1929 100% bonuses were also paid, making the total 402.5% over the nine years which saw spectacular failures of shipping companies like Royal Mail and Western Counties. Despite these payments assets fell only from £451,890 in 1924 to £331,477 in 1927, £285,882 in 1930 and were still at £233,771 in the final accounts when the company was wound up. In the years 1923 to 1930 the profit and loss account ranged between £45,741 and £24,529.

No ships had been acquired at inflated wartime prices. Southdown waited before buying what would be its last ship, *Rustington* (3), delivered by William Gray and Co. in December 1924 and likely paid for from the cash reserves, giving a three-ship fleet. The year 1926 saw *Dallington* go to owners in Trieste for £11,000. Herbert Symondson died in October 1928 and the board was strengthened by the appointment of another son of Thomas Bell, Arthur Bell (1882-1963), and Frederick Schooling, Herbert Symondson's brother-in-law and a director of the Prudential Assurance Co. Ltd.

The Great Depression followed the Wall Street collapse on 29th October 1929. Trade slackened and by 1934 was at 77% of the 1929 figure. An increasing number of ships were laid up, at times totalling more than two million tons in UK ports alone. *Novington* was laid up in the Fal from 2nd May to September 1930, and *Rustington* (3) lay in the Clyde after arriving at Greenock on 1st June 1931 until sold. However, with laid up ships in every port it was clear that worse was to come.

In 1931, with no sign of improving conditions, the directors acted. The ships were sold, *Novington* (2) on 26th February at Cardiff for £14,000 and *Rustington* (3) on 14th September for £18,000; good prices for the period and a full recovery of their value, £31,728. In November 1931 Southdown was placed in liquidation. The accounts in 1930 were in good order, so in November the paid up capital of £72,688 was returned to shareholders and by May 1932 a further £26 2s 2d. had been distributed for each £10 share. The reserves were such that the company could well have survived and traded through the Second World War, but the future was not clear and the directors made a wise decision in protecting the shareholders' assets. *Novington* (2) was the last ship to survive, going for scrap in 1961 as the Turkish *Ismet*, outliving Bell, Symondson and Co. who were last recorded in the Post Office Directory for London in 1954.

Fleet list

1. VERNON 1892-1894 Raised quarter deck iron
O.N. 89774 1,461g 935n 1,950d
243.0 x 34.0 x 17.9 feet.
C.2-cyl. by Blair and Co. Ltd., Stockton-on-Tees (31 and 58 x 36 inches); 144 NHP.
11.3.1884: Launched by Thomas Turnbull and Sons, Whitby (Yard No. 95) for Thomas Smailes and Son, Whitby as JOHN STEVENSON
1892: Acquired by S.V. Symondson, London and renamed VERNON.

17.1.1894: Wrecked at Bernathen near Libau whilst on a voyage from the River Tyne to Libau with a cargo of coal.

2. INVERMAY 1893-1896 Single deck iron
O.N. 89775 1,436g 916n 1,930d
240.0 x 34.0 x 17.8 feet.
C.2-cyl. by Blair and Co. Ltd., Stockton-on-Tees (32 and 60 x 39 inches); 154 NHP.
24.5.1884: Launched by Thomas Turnbull and Sons, Whitby (Yard No. 97) for the Steamship Invermay Co. Ltd. (Stoddart

Brothers, managers), Liverpool as INVERMAY.
1888: Managers became Thomas Turnbull and Sons, Whitby.
1893: Acquired by S.V. Symondson, London.
1896: Sold to Becchi & Calcagno, Savona, Italy and renamed ARMONIA.
1900: Sold to Aznar y Compañia, Bilbao, Spain and renamed AXPE.
1902: Sold to Compañia Vasco Cantabrica de Navegacion (Adolfo Pardo, manager), Bilbao.

1904: Manager became Fernando Pereda.
1914: Sold to Compañia Espanola de Navegacion (Ulpiano Torre, manager), Bilbao.
1916: Sold to S.A. Navegacion Espanola (Kendall Park, manager), Barcelona, Spain and renamed GERONA.
6.12.1916: Captured and sunk by the German submarine UC 21 in position 49.04 north by 06.20 west whilst on a voyage from Oporto to Cardiff with a cargo of pit props.

3. GEORGIA 1894-1902 Raised quarter deck
O.N. 89472 1,732g 1,066n 2,450d
261.5 x 36.8 x 18.2 feet.
C. 2-cyl. by Black, Hawthorn and Co., Gateshead (32 and 60 x 39 inches); 675 IHP.
30.3.1885: Launched by William Gray and Co., West Hartlepool (Yard No. 292) for their own account as GEORGIA.
1894: Acquired by S.V. Symondson, London.
2.12.1897: Transferred to the Southdown Steamship Co. Ltd. (Bell, Symondson and Co., managers), London.
1902: Sold to Ångfartygs A/B Kattegat (Nils Th. Pyk, manager), Helsingborg, Sweden.
1906: Manager became H. Swensson.
1916: Sold to Rederi A/B Kistransport (Lloyd Lundström, manager), Helsingborg.
1919: Sold to Rederi A/B Vala (Oscar A. Borjesson, manager), Helsingborg and renamed LORD.
1920: Transferred to Rederi A/B Amaryllis (Oscar A. Borjesson, manager), Helsingborg.
1921: Transferred to Rederi A/B Alfa (Oscar A. Borjesson, manager), Helsingborg.
1929: Sold to Rederi A/B Strandvik (N.P. Lundh, manager), Landskrona, Sweden and renamed ARNE.
1934: Sold to Rederi A/B Arne (T. Lundh, manager), Helsingborg.
1938: Manager became Morgan Wedlin.
1939: Sold to E. Lass, J. Lambut, J. Aguraiuja & Rederi A/B Arne (Morgan Wedlin, manager), Tallinn, Estonia and renamed AGU.
5.12.1939: Sailed from the River Tyne for Gothenburg with a cargo of coal and disappeared, believed to have been mined in the North Sea.
7.2.1940: Posted missing at Lloyd's.

4. RUSTINGTON (1) 1897-1906 Single deck
O.N. 108258 2,185g 1,377n 3,600d
288.0 x 42.0 x 19.6 feet.
T. 3-cyl by George Clark Ltd., Sunderland (22, 35 and 57.5 x 39 inches); 208 NHP.
27.8.1897: Launched by Osbourne, Graham and Co., Sunderland (Yard No. 104) for the Southdown Steamship Co.

The former *Georgia* under the Swedish flag as *Lord* at Preston, sometime between 1925 and 1929. Note the style of painting the name, probably in the Swedish national colours of yellow and blue, which was a trademark of ships managed by Oscar Borjesson of Helsingborg. *[Harry Stewart/J. & M. Clarkson]*

Rustington (1) completed at Sunderland in 1897. *[Nigel Farrell collection]*

Ltd. (Bell, Symondson and Co., managers), London as RUSTINGTON.
10.1897: Completed.
1906: Sold to the Portsea Steamship Co. Ltd. (McNeil, Hinde and Co., managers), Cardiff and renamed PORTSMOUTH.
1912: Sold to Trelleborgs Ångfartygs Nya A/B (F.D. Malmros, manager), Trelleborg, Sweden and renamed WILLIAM.
1916: Sold to Olaf Orvig, Bergen, Norway and renamed GUSTAV VIGELAND.
4.9.1916: Wrecked on the Knavestone Rock, near the Longstone, whilst on a voyage from Archangel to London with a cargo of timber.

5. NOVINGTON (1) 1899-1911 Single deck
O.N. 110112 2,538g 1,617n 4,350d
313.0 x 44.5 x 20.6 feet.
T. 3-cyl. by Blair and Co. Ltd., Stockton-on-Tees (23, 37.5 and 61.5 x 39 inches); 244 NHP.

29.3.1899: Launched by Richardson, Duck and Co., Stockton-on-Tees (Yard No. 503) for the Southdown Steamship Co. Ltd. (Bell, Symondson and Co., managers), London as NOVINGTON.
5.1899: Completed.
1911: Sold to Rederi A/B Helsingborg (N.C. Corfitzon, manager), Helsingborg, Sweden and renamed CONSUL OLSSON.
2.1918: Company bought by Rederi A/B Transatlantic (Gunnar Carlsson, manager), Gothenburg, Sweden and ship renamed SALEN.
6.1921: Transferred to Rederi A/B Transatlantic (Gunnar Carlsson, manager), Gothenburg.
7.1921: Sold to Aug. Bolten, Wm. Miller's Nachfolger, Hamburg, Germany and renamed ATHALWIN.
6.1923: Reverted to Rederi A/B Transatlantic (Gunnar Carlsson, manager), Gothenburg and renamed SALEN.
23.4.1925: Sold to Rederi A/B Helsingborg

Above: *Novington* of 1899. *[Nigel Farrell collection]*

(Otto Hillerström), Helsingborg and renamed
ARGOS.
22.6.1925: Stranded at Cat Island,
Newfoundland, on first voyage for the new
owners from Argentia to Miramichi in ballast.
Declared a constructive total loss and
abandoned.

6. DALLINGTON 1900-1926 Single deck.
O.N. 112744 2,534g 1,613n 4,350d
313.1 x 44.6 x 20.6 feet.
T. 3-cyl. by Blair and Co. Ltd., Stockton-on-
Tees (23, 37.5 and 61.5 x 39 inches); 1,150
IHP.
13.7.1900: Launched by Richardson, Duck
and Co., Stockton-on-Tees (Yard No. 515) the
Southdown Steamship Co. Ltd. (Bell,
Symondson and Co., managers), London as
DALLINGTON.
8.1900: Completed.
1926: Sold to Slobodna Plovidba Topiæ D.D.
(Ant. Topic), Trieste, Italy and renamed
SERAFIN TOPIC.
1933: Broken up by Societa Italiana Ernesto
Breda, Venice.

Her sister *Dallington* was completed in 1900. *[Nigel Farrell collection]*

7. LULLINGTON 1903-1917 Single deck
O.N. 118309 2,816g 1,821n 4,850d
323.0 x 46.6 x 21.4 feet.
T. 3-cyl. by Blair and Co. Ltd., Stockton-on-
Tees (23, 38 and 62.5 x 42 inches); 1,050
IHP.
9.7.1903: Launched by Richardson, Duck
and Co., Stockton-on-Tees (Yard No. 550)
for the Southdown Steamship Co. Ltd. (Bell,
Symondson and Co., managers), London as
LULLINGTON.
8.1903: Completed.
8.2.1917: Mined and sunk three miles east of
the Royal Sovereign Light Vessel and ten
miles south west of Hastings whilst on a
voyage as an Admiralty collier from Blyth to
Rouen with a cargo of coal. The mine was
laid on the previous day by the German
submarine UC 47.

Below: *Lullington* seen here in the Avon was mined in 1917. *[George Scott collection]*

8. JEVINGTON 1905-1917 Single deck
O.N. 120584 2,747g 1,738n 4,950d
331.2 x 47.5 x 20.0 feet.
T. 3-cyl. by Blair and Co. Ltd., Stockton-on-Tees (23, 38 and 62.5 x 42 inches); 1,400 IHP.
1.7.1905: Launched by Richardson, Duck and Co., Stockton-on-Tees (Yard No. 564) the Southdown Steamship Co. Ltd. (Bell, Symondson and Co., managers), London as JEVINGTON.
7.1905: Completed.
23.1.1917: Torpedoed and sunk by the German submarine U 43 52 miles north west by half west from Cape Ortegal in position 44.08 north by 09.00 west whilst on a voyage from Rosario to Rochefort with a cargo of wheat.

9. RUSTINGTON (2) 1909-1917 Single deck
O.N. 129057 3,071g 1,900n 5,450d
340.0 x 49.1 x 21.0 feet.
T. 3-cyl. by Blair and Co. Ltd., Stockton-on-Tees (23, 39 and 64 x 45 inches); 1,800 IHP, 8.5 knots.
24.11.1909: Launched by Richardson, Duck and Co., Stockton-on-Tees (Yard No. 606) for the Southdown Steamship Co. Ltd. (Bell, Symondson and Co., managers), London as RUSTINGTON.
12.1909: Completed.
25.7.1917: Torpedoed and sunk by the German submarine U 54 235 miles west by south of Ushant in position 46.26 north by 10.00 west whilst on a voyage from Aguilas to Cardiff with a cargo of iron ore.

10. NOVINGTON (2) 1912-1931 Single deck
O.N. 132729 3,442g 2,100n 6,000d
362.0 x 50.0 x 21.6 feet.
T. 3-cyl. by Blair and Co. Ltd., Stockton-on-Tees (25, 41 and 67 x 45 inches); 1,950 IHP; 9 knots.
4.5.1912: Launched by Richardson, Duck and Co. Ltd., Stockton-on-Tees (Yard No. 625) for the Southdown Steamship Co. Ltd. (Bell, Symondson and Co., managers), London as NOVINGTON.
6.1912: Completed.
1931: Sold to M. Frangos, Chios, Greece and renamed IOANNIS FRANCOS.
1941: Transferred to the Sirios Steamship Co. Ltd. (Marinos & Frangos Ltd., managers), Athens, Greece.
1954: Sold to Resit Eskin ve Ramiz Yilmaz, Istanbul, Turkey and renamed RAMIZ.
1956: Sold to Faik Zeren Vapurlari Isletmesi, Istanbul and renamed ISMET.
25.5.1961: Arrived at Piraeus to be broken up by Sideroboriki Co. Ltd.
8.1961: Work began.

11. RUSTINGTON (3) 1924-1931 Single deck
O.N. 148519 3,734g 2,274n
360.0 x 51.0 x 22.9 feet.
T. 3-cyl by Central Marine Engine Works, West Hartlepool (25, 40.3 and 67 x 45 inches); 332 NHP.

Jevington completed in 1905. *[Nigel Farrell collection]*

Above: *Rustington* (2). *[Nigel Farrell collection]*
Below: *Novington* (2) served as *Collier 152* and Expeditionary Force transport *D1206* in the First World War. *[Nigel Farrell collection]*

10.11.1924: Launched by William Gray and Co. Ltd., West Hartlepool (Yard No. 966) for Southdown Steamship Co. Ltd. (Bell, Symondson and Co., managers), London as RUSTINGTON.

12.1924: Completed.
1931: Sold to Stamatios G. Embiricos, Athens, Greece and renamed IOANNIS M EMBIRICOS.
5.2.1941: Bombed and machine gunned by

One of two ships briefly managed by Bell, Symondson and Co. for the Shipping Controller, the former *War Parrot* is seen as Bank Line's *Yoseric*. [Ships in Focus]

a Fw 200 Condor of KG 40 in position 55.41 north by 12.26 west after losing convoy SC 20 in bad weather whilst on a voyage from Montreal to Preston with 1,700 standards of Columbian pine. The crew abandoned the ship and were rescued by HM corvette PICOTEE and HM trawler LADY MADELEINE.
8.2.1941: Derelict sunk.

Managed for the Shipping Controller

M1. WAR PARROT 1918-1919 B class standard, two decks
O.N. 142605 5,240g 3,221g 8,075d
400.0 x 52.4 x 28.5 feet.
T. 3-cyl. by Harland and Wolff Ltd., Glasgow (27, 44 and 73 x 48 inches); 2,500 IHP, 11 knots.
27.5.1918: Launched by Sir James Laing and Sons Ltd., Sunderland (Yard No. 671) for the Shipping Controller (Bell, Symondson and Co., managers), London as WAR PARROT.
7.1918: Completed.
1919: Sold to Bank Line Ltd. (Andrew Weir and Co., managers), London and renamed YOSERIC.
1936: Sold to Glenfield Syndicate Ltd., London and renamed ENA G.
1936: Sold to the Uskside Steamship Co. Ltd. (Richard W. Jones and Co., managers), Newport and tendered for scrapping under the 'Scrap and Build' scheme against the USKSIDE (2,706/1937).
1936: Broken up by John Cashmore Ltd., Newport.

War Pigeon in Italian ownership as *Carignano*: note the lattice derricks. [Roy Fenton collection]

M2. WAR PIGEON 1918-1919 B class standard, two decks
O.N. 142617 5,272g 3,203n 8,075d
400.0 x 52.4 x 28.4 feet.
T. 3-cyl. by Harland and Wolff Ltd., Glasgow (27, 44 and 73 x 48 inches); 2,500 IHP, 11 knots.
10.6.1918: Launched by Ropner and Sons Ltd., Stockton-on-Tees (Yard No. 525) for the Shipping Controller (Bell, Symondson and Co., managers), London as WAR PIGEON.
9.1918: Completed.
1919: Sold to Phs van Ommeren, Rotterdam, Holland.
1919: Sold to Societa Anonima Lloyd Sabaudo, Genoa, Italy and renamed CARIGNANO.
1932: Transferred to 'Italia' (Flotte Riunite, Cosulich, Lloyd Sabaudo N.G.I.).
1937: Transferred to Lloyd Triestino S.A. di Navigazione, Trieste, Italy.

1942: Bareboat chartered to the Japanese Government and renamed TEIYU MARU.
9.1943: Seized by Japanese Government.
13.11.1944: Bombed and sunk by US Navy aircraft in Manila Bay during the Battle of Leyte Gulf.

M3. CLÄRE HUGO STINNES 1 1919-1921 Two decks
O.N. 143084 4,984g 3,099n 7,820d
383.8 x 51.7 x 26.8 feet.
T. 3-cyl. by Bremer Vulkan Schiffbau & Maschinenfabrik, Vegesack, Germany (24, 39 and 64 x 43.5 feet); 1,700 IHP, 9 knots.
7.3.1910: Launched by Bremer Vulkan Schiffbau & Maschinenfabrik, Vegesack (Yard No. 533) for Hugo Stinnes, Mülheim/Ruhr, German as CLÄRE HUGO STINNES 1.
6.4.1910: Delivered.
1912: Transferred to Hugo Stinnes G.m.b.H., Mülheim/Ruhr.

Cläre Hugo Stinnes 1 was managed for the Shipping Controller from 1919 to 1921. [Fritz Vonarb collection]

12.11.1912: Transferred to 'Cläre Hugo Stinnes 1' Dampschiffahrts-G.m.b.H. (K.R. Hugo Stinnes G.m.b.H., managers), Hamburg.
23.3.1919: Surrendered to the Shipping Controller (Bell, Symondson and Co., managers), London.
1921: Sold to Atlantic Transportation Co. Ltd., Montreal, Canada and renamed PHILIP T. DODGE.
1946: Sold to Chung Hsing Steamship Co. Ltd. (Chung Hsing Coal Mining Co. Ltd.), Shanghai, China and renamed FOO HSING.
6.5.1947: Stranded at Ockseu in position 24.59 north by 119.28 east whilst on a voyage from Bangkok to Shanghai with a cargo of rice.
1.6.1947: Refloated badly damaged, declared a constructive total loss and sold to Hong Kong shipbreakers.

M4. PERA 1919-1921 Spar deck
O.N. 118710/143076* 4,035g 2,605n 6,640d
360.0 x 50.2 x 17.0 feet.
T. 3-cyl. by D. and W. Henderson and Co. Ltd., Glasgow (25, 41 and 67 x 45 inches); 2,200 IHP, 10 knots.
13.7.1905: Launched by D. and W. Henderson and Co. Ltd., Glasgow (Yard No. 446) for La Commerciale Steam Navigation Co. Ltd. (Frank C. Strick and Co. Ltd., managers), London as ARMANISTAN.
8.1905: Completed.
22.1.1906: Sold to Union Dampfschiffs Reederi 'Union' A.G., Hamburg, Germany and renamed WELLGUNDE.
23.1.1912: Sold to Continentale Rhederei A.G., Hamburg and renamed HEIMFELD.
18.10.1913: Sold to Deutsche Levante Linie, Hamburg.
24.2.1914: Renamed PERA.
22.3.1919: Surrendered to the Shipping Controller (Bell, Symondson and Co., managers), London.
1921: Sold to the Bolton Steam Shipping Co. Ltd. (F. Bolton and Co., managers),

London and renamed RUBENS (the name RIBERA was initially chosen).
1927: Sold to Perrakis I. Corcodilos, Piraeus, Greece and renamed IOANNIS CORCODILOS.
26.12.1933: Arrived at Savona, Italy to be broken up, having been sold for £4,100.
1934: Work began.

*PERA was mistakenly given a new official number in 1919.

M5. SAKKARAH 1919-1921 Shelter deck
O.N. 143322 4,670g 3,010n 8,482d
400.0 x 52.0 x 27.0 feet.
T. 3-cyl. by the Wallsend Slipway Co. Ltd., Wallsend-on-Tyne (27, 45 and 75 x 48 inches); 2,500 IHP, 10 knots.
3.8.1906: Launched by Armstrong, Whitworth and Co. Ltd., Newcastle-upon-Tyne (Yard No. 779) for Deutsche-Dampfschiffahrts Gesellschaft 'Kosmos', Hamburg, Germany as SAKKARAH.
12.9.1906: Completed.
28.6.1919: Surrendered to the Shipping Controller (Bell, Symondson and Co., managers), London.
1921: Sold to Alexander Shipping Co. Ltd. (Capper, Alexander and Co., managers), London and renamed CHARLBURY.
1935: Sold to St Quentin Shipping Co. Ltd. (B. and S. Shipping Co. Ltd.), Cardiff and tendered under the 'Scrap and Build' scheme against the ST HELENA (4,313/ 1936).
22.2.1936: Arrived at Osaka to be broken up.

Above: Armanistan seen here as the Ioannis Corcodilos was managed by Bell, Symondson and Co. as the Pera from 1919 to 1921. [Nigel Farrell]
Below: Charlbury, the former Sakkarah, managed from 1919 to 1921 when she was bought by the Alexander Shipping Co. Ltd. and renamed. [Roy Fenton collection]

BOWATERS REVISITED

A feature on the ships of papermakers Bowaters in 'Record' 5 stirred up much interest in the company. The scrapping of the last survivor from the fleet in 2003 has prompted a revisit.

Last of the Bowaters   **Peter Newall**
The last of the ships owned by the once-mighty Bowater paper company was broken up in Latvia in 2003. The 4,045gt Norwegian vessel *Norskald* was built as *Elizabeth Bowater* in 1958 and was probably the sole survivor of Britain's large ocean-going cargo fleet of the 1950s.

At the time of her completion, Bowater was the largest newsprint manufacturer in the world with a landmark head office in Knightsbridge, London and paper mills in the UK, Canada and the USA. The company owed its success to the dynamism of Sir Eric Vansittart Bowater who had led the company since 1926. In 1955 the Bowater Steamship Co. Ltd. was established to control the transportation of raw materials and newspaper print and in its heyday had a fleet of twelve ships, most of which were named after members of the Bowater family. Their distinctive colour scheme consisted of a green hull with yellow funnels bearing the Bowater rebus logo, which is a B-shaped bow over blue and white lines representing water.

Elizabeth Bowater was the first of six handsome ships with a streamlined funnel and superstructure slightly aft of amidships. Designed to carry pulpwood between Britain and Scandinavia, she also served the Bowater plants in Canada and North America and was ice-strengthened so that she could operate year-round. The holds were built without pillars or obstructions which might damage the rolls of newspaper print. She was also the first British ship to be fitted with a Pleuger Aktiv rudder which had a small propeller driven by a 150hp motor. This extraordinary device improved her manoeuvrability in confined waters.

After the death of Sir Eric in 1962, the company underwent considerable change and by the early 1970s the Bowater fleet was sold off. *Elizabeth Bowater* was bought by Wimpey (Marine) Ltd., which converted her into a drill ship. The rest of her career was spent as a research and soil sampling

ship and despite a large rig amidships was little changed externally. Of the remaining sisters four were scrapped in the 1980s whilst the former 1960-built *Phyllis Bowater* only went to Indian breakers a few years ago. Meanwhile, Bowater's North American operation de-merged from its British parent in 1984 and continues under the Bowater logo as one of the continent's largest paper makers whilst in Britain the Bowater name disappeared when the company became Rexam in 1995.

Top: Elizabeth Bowater on trials in 1958.
Bottom: The Pleuger Aktiv rudder fitted at Leith in May 1958.
[Both Peter Newall collection]

Ian Howatson, whose father worked on Bowater's ships, photographed *Norskald*, ex-*Pholas*, ex-*Wimpey Sealab*, ex-*Elizabeth Bowater* at a shipbreakers' yard in Esbjerg. Although the ship was rust-streaked on the outside, Ian reports she was in remarkably good condition on the inside. It was almost like the crew had just been asked to get off the ship; sauce bottles still on the tables in the cafeteria, clothes left in the lockers in the cabins, and there was even a tray on the bridge with cups and a tea pot ready to be used. Two pieces of Bowater china, a milk jug and cream jug, remained. The Bowater's funnel emblem could be clearly seen on her funnel.

The ship had been laid up at Haugesund in March 2000, her final job being geological drilling in the Straits of Gibraltar for a planned tunnel to link Africa to Europe. In November 2002 she was bought by the Danish breakers Smedegaarden and towed to Esjberg. Smedegaarden specialise in breaking fishing boats and small coasters, and *Norskald* would have been its biggest project. However, she was sold on to Liepaja Metalurgs, Liepaja, Latvia and left Esbjerg on 6th June 2003. She arrived in Liepaja on 14th June and work commenced just three days later.

Round the world on *Nicolas Bowater*: a steward's tale

Pete Lindstrom

Bowater's paid us £12 a month higher than any other company plus lots of overtime. We were painting the interior of the ship day and night during her maiden voyage. It was good money in those days and we all had our very own cabins with complete privacy. It was very unusual especially in a British ship. The company spared no expense when it came to maintenance (there was a reason for this) and she was a very modern up-to-date ship. But that was the bright side of things. Unfortunately, the *Nicolas Bowater* turned out to be the most miserable, unhappy ship that any of us had ever sailed on.

In June 1958, I was sent up to Denny of Dumbarton to work on the new ship. Not many of us had ever heard of Bowaters: most of us were Cunard men. We were to get her ready for her maiden voyage. We worked on her as a shore gang for about six weeks before signing on. Apparently Denny were way behind on their delivery date and everything turned into a rush job: this was to be the flagship of the fleet to be shown off to all Bowater's customers around the world, and now she was late.

She failed her sea trials twice before she was approved. Each time we came back it was another week in the dockyard. It was good for the crew, as it gave us more time ashore with our girlfriends. We finally set sail for Sweden and there just off the coast experienced the first problem. The first mate fell down one of the hatches and injured his back. A helicopter came out to meet us and took him ashore.

We returned to the UK to prepare her for the main trip. It was unusual to return to Scotland with a lot of engineers running all over the ship before we set sail for Corner Brook, Newfoundland.

For many weeks before signing on we had been told that the Bowater service was to be just three month trips up and down the US east coast and then she would return to the UK.

In the winter of 1958 we headed across the North Atlantic. The first couple of days seemed to be quite normal, with the weather typical for that time of year. But just as we got to the point of no return, south of Greenland, the engines seized. Without power we were at the mercy of the weather and the heavy swells were rocking us in an unusual manner. We were lucky being able to maintain steerage way by using emergency generators that provided electrical power to the steering gear. This enabled us to keep her head into the wind without her getting knocked sideways by the heavy swells.

We drifted around as we waited for a rendezvous with a deep-sea tug that towed us to the Royal Canadian Navy shipyard in Halifax, Nova Scotia. Here it was like ants on an apple core. Marine engineers and turbine setters from Denny were flown out to Halifax, and worked day and night with Canadian engineers for three and a half weeks. They had to remove the skylight to take the engines out of the ship. Replacement engine parts were flown in from Scotland.

The lubricating system had been contaminated with metal swarf that had been left inside the engine at the factory. The oil galleries and the bearings, being starved, got so hot they seized. But we were lucky: we could have had an engine room fire on our hands.

The ship had been built with a number of first class cabins, or I should say suites, to cater for Bowater's guests. They were very much the same standard as a first class cabin on the Queens. We in the catering department were there to provide the entertainment for cocktail and dinner parties which would continue for almost a year.

I mentioned earlier that we assumed that the ship was to do three or four runs up and down the US east coast delivering newsprint from Corner Brook and then she would go back to the UK, when we would all get a couple of weeks leave before the next trip. Well, after our second trip down the east coast when arriving back at Corner Brook we got a shock. There laying on the quay was our new cargo marked for the *Nicolas Bowater* but also marked Cape Town, Port Elizabeth, East London, Durban, Mombasa. The crew began to get angry at this. Not because it meant going to Africa, but because they had been lied to by the management. Three

Nicolas Bowater. [Ships in Focus]

or four of the crew visited doctors and were able to get notes saying that they physically couldn't handle the African heat and so they were able to go home. They were replaced with Canadians just before we sailed.

Crossing the Atlantic on our way to Africa, one of the men that worked in the engine room became ill and died of heat exhaustion; he was in his late forties. We buried him at sea just off the west coast of Africa. It was a full white dress ceremony, with the ship stopped. He was draped in a Red Duster. It was a very sad day for all: no-one talked, we just looked at each other in disbelief.

Five days later we arrived at Cape Town and the rest of the trip went without incident. We sailed up the east coast putting into Durban, Beira, Lorenco Marques, Tanga, Mombasa, and passed through the Suez Canal without any problems. As soon as we turned due west heading for Gibraltar our spirits began to pick up: we were going home! Sorry Charlie, not this time! We just couldn't believe it. As soon as we passed Gibraltar she headed north west and we were on our way back to Corner Brook. The lads were just about ready to start a mutiny.

The word from the top was, we'll just be picking up a cargo for the UK and we'll be home in about fifteen days don't worry about it. But arriving back at Corner Brook, there it was, our new cargo marked Melbourne, Sydney, Brisbane! The lads were just about ready to kill, especially the married guys. We had been lied to again.

Again some of them got Canadian doctors' notes and had to wait for a UK bound ship that would take them home. Some of the men had written to their wives telling them to file a complaint with Bowater's head office. Then, all of a sudden, our mail stopped. It was being controlled and intercepted. No one was allowed to send any mail ashore in Panama, and no shore leave was permitted.

We went on strike in Sydney. We just took off for three or four days and travelled around the town. We found the Seaman's Union office, looking for some protection, but the office had been abandoned. The media got wind of the trouble on the ship, and when we got back there were about twenty reporters waiting to interview us about abusive treatment of the crew. They saved our bacon: all of a sudden, our sins where forgiven and they laid on all kinds of outings and bus trips for us.

On the homeward bound voyage, we faced retaliation. After arriving back in the UK and signing off we found that they had deleted six months' overtime pay, overtime that had already been earned on her maiden voyage.

We had a couple of happy moments on some of the voyages. After midnight, when all was quiet, one of the mates would allow us up on the bridge and let us man the helm for a couple of hours at a time. It was a big novelty to us catering wimps that did not qualify to work on deck. We would hold competitions to see who could steer the straightest course. Behind the helm and in the chart room there was a course recording machine. It copied almost every move you made with the helm. And so it was, 'OK lads, place your bets.' One night while at the helm, the old man walked right onto the bridge, he walked right passed me and didn't bat an eyelid. It was pitch black except for the compass with its dim glow. I was sweating!

FROM THE BOSUN'S LOCKER
John Clarkson

We are a little bit short of space to stow the bosun's locker in this issue, so to begin we will report on our reader's deliberations on past problems.

03/29. This damaged sailing vessel has been identified as *Polykarp*, but John Naylon has serious doubts about this. A photograph in his collection of *Polykarp* at Bristol shows she has a different hull form from the vessel in 03/29. John also points out that the newspaper reports state that the *Polykarp* 'had a portion of her port bulwarks swept away' and noted 'the splintered condition of her bulwarks', yet these do not appear in the photograph. Further suggestions for the identity of 03/29 are therefore welcome.

01/33. Nigel Farrell, Dave Hocquard and George Robinson are convinced that this photograph depicts a steamer belonging to John Wetherall of Goole. From comparisons with photos available, especially in Charles Hill's collection, she is either the *Hessle* or *Saltmarshe* of 1907, sisters built by William Pickersgill and Son, Sunderland. Indeed, the background could be this very shipyard. The only difference between 01/33 and certified photographs of *Saltmarshe* and *Hessle* is that the latter show just one boom on the foremast, whilst 01/33 has two, one forward and one aft. It could be that this was later removed, or stowed against the mast whilst in service. *Saltmarshe* was sold to the Lancashire and Yorkshire Railway when only two months old, and under their successors continued to trade out of Goole until 1932. *Hessle* remained with Wetherall until 1917 when sold to Swansea owners. She was sold to Germany in 1929 and as *Norden* survived until broken up in 1953. Of the editor's suggestion that she might be Swedish, the less said the better: Wincks actually had a white letter W on their funnels; that on Wetherall's funnel was dark.

02/33. Dave Hocquard has identified this vessel as the steamer *Carterside* of Newcastle-upon-Tyne; he has a similar print the back of which carries a note that she was arriving at Littlehampton on Wednesday 9th June 1932 with 300 standards of wood. Details of her career are below.

CARTERSIDE 1924-1936
O.N. 140288 824g 380n   195.0 x 30.0 x 12.0 feet
T. 3-cyl. by John Dickinson and Sons Ltd., Sunderland; 119 NHP, 580 IHP, 10 knots.
4.1917: Completed by Bartram and Sons Ltd., Sunderland (Yard No 240).
24.4.1917: Registered in the ownership of the Town Line (London) Ltd. (George F. Harrison of Harrison, Sons and Co., manager), London as ENNISTOWN.
31.1.1922: Sold to Philip Angel and Arthur J. Godert, Cardiff.
10.2.1922: Sold to the Triumph Steamship Co. (1922) Ltd. (Richard Angel, manager), Cardiff.
22.5.1922: Renamed SUNNYCROFT.
16.10.1923: Sold to the Side Shipping Co. Ltd. (Connell and Grace Ltd., managers), Newcastle-upon-Tyne.
2.1.1924: Renamed CARTERSIDE
26.8.1936: Sold to John Stewart and Company Shipping Ltd., Glasgow.
15.9.1936: Renamed YEWKYLE.
15.1.1945: Sunk in collision with an unknown vessel, believed to

be the SYLVIA BEALE (1,040/1938), off Harwich in position 52.09 north by 01.50 east whilst on a voyage from Blyth to Portsmouth with a cargo of coal. *19.1.1945:* Register closed.

03/34. The location has been convincingly identified as Foyers on Loch Ness, part of the Caledonian Canal. The quay, railway and cranes were built in the 1890s to serve a hydro-electric scheme which harnessed the Falls of Foyer to provide power for an aluminium smelter. Thanks to Ian Ramsay, and George Gardner who provided documentary and pictorial evidence for the location. Indeed, George provided copies of photographs from Glasgow University Archives (see overleaf) of the topsail schooner *Regent* taken at the jetty on another occasion but from the same angle.

The identity of the single hatch coaster remains a mystery, but may well be one of the fleet of John G. Stewart of Glasgow, which carried 'Loch' names, and which was associated with aluminium producers. The photo from Glasgow, reproduced right, may be an earlier view - there is only one derrick and the quay wall has not been clad with stone.

Chemical versus digital
In the last issue I commented on the growing problems of obtaining supplies of chemicals and how photographers to some extent are being forced down the digital path.

Two readers, David Atherton and Mark Teadham, have written in with details of suppliers who they find to be helpful and for the benefit of any readers who still do their own processing I will give the basic details.

Jacobs in Bold Street, Liverpool (0151 709 3733) stock paper and chemical supplies, also enlarger lamps. They also have a shop in Manchester. Also in Bold Street are Sampsons who carry smaller stocks. In Market Street, Bolton there is Mathers of Lancashire (01204 522186) who stock a good range of Ilford black and white products and are David's sole supplier of 35mm bulk film. They also supply by mail order without high delivery charges.

At the other end of the country is Mr Cad in Windmill Road, Croydon (020 8684 8282), with a very helpful and knowledgeable staff who recently supplied 10 litre drums of chemicals overnight for a £6.50 delivery and insurance charge. Retro Photographic (08452 262647) supply film, paper and chemicals to most formulations going back to the 1920s, even the raw chemicals for those who would like to try coating their own glass plates. Silverprint Ltd. in Camden, North London (0207 6200 844) is worth knowing.

Foyers Jetty, Loch Ness. *[Glasgow University Archives UGD347/21/53/19]*

Thank you David and Mark for this information which has been built up from experience. Keep up the good work with the black and white - your quality pictures of today should still be around in many years when colour, and perhaps digital, may have faded away.

Museums and their charges
Have you ever had dealings with museums in the UK over the supply of photographs and the use of them in publications? How have you been treated and what is your opinion of their services and charges?

Generally we find the staff to be most helpful but not all are knowledgeable - a request for the *Queen of Bermuda* in the Tyne resulted in a photo of a ship with 'three big things on top in a river', as the lady put it. The ship turned out to be the *Queen*

1/34: The only note on the reverse of this photo is "Liverpool Docks". Looking at the sheds in the background this is probably correct. The name of the ship is only just illegible. Ahead is what may be a Pacific Steam Navigation liner - *Orbita, Orduna,* or if early in the war, the *Oropesa.*
I am sure someone will again accuse the old bosun of going soft, but so what, surely in his 65th year he is allowed occassionally to make it easy for the readers. Too many hard problems and some readers lose interest. Now have a look at the others lined up for you - perhaps not so easy.

Gerrit J. de Boer in Holland has supplied the first two pictures for identification which we are using in this issue of 'Record'. Perhaps both are Dutch?

2/34: There is nothing on the back of this photograph except the glue which held it in what was probably a family photo album. The only identifying feature is the five pointed star on the funnel. There are straps around the funnel but close examination of the print makes me think it is otherwise plain with a black top. The clipper bow makes her look old but the bridge may be enclosed.

3/34: Normally we would not include a picture of an unknown ship with a plain black hull and buff funnel - there were too many of them. This one is slightly different: she has what look like six large open ports in her side - two forward and four at her stern. The funnel may have a narrow black top but this could be soot. The name definitely has six letters and in the foreground, but not included, is a bum-boat or small loaded cargo lighter. Does anyone recognise the background?

4/34: David Whiteside asks for help identifying the vessel in the accompanying photograph taken by Michael Cassar in Malta. The name *A Cecche..* is being painted up on what may once have been a British coaster.

Mary in New York - not quite what we wanted. But the big problem is charges. Two images obtained recently from a museum in the south east, along with reproduction rights, came with a bill for £111.70 plus £19.55 VAT. They even charged £1.70 for postage. To clarify, the charge was for a CD bearing two images with permission to reproduce them up to full-page size in a publication with a print run of no more than one thousand. Talking to the same museum some years ago we were told that they, the staff, were there to preserve the artefacts in their museum for posterity. Sorry chum, but not much point if no one is ever going to see the material and few publishers will use their material at these prices. I know museums need funding but surely it would be better to encourage publishers such as ourselves to make these pictures more widely available rather than just leaving them hidden away 'for posterity'. I rest my case and look forward to your comments.

EVERY PICTURE TELLS A STORY

Photographs of ships with their decks piled high with timber are common enough, but having decks piled high with trucks is unusual to say the least. With the vehicles piled higgledy-piggledy, it is a far cry from the vehicle carriers of the twenty-first century, and the parking leaves something to be desired.

It has been suggested that the cargo consists of army lorries, destined for Italy's brutal campaign in Abyssinia. The date is between 1937, when the ship took the name *Styliani*, and the repainting of her and other ships in wartime grey or neutrality markings, probably late 1939. The invaluable Voyage Record Cards, which are part of the Lloyd's Collection at the Guildhall Library in London, show that she may well have made such a voyage late in 1937, but this was too late for the main campaign, which culminated in the annexation of Abyssinia as Ethiopia in May 1936. About 15th December 1937 *Styliani* departed from La Spezia and passed Port Said on 29th December. Her destination is not recorded, but could well have been a port in Ethiopia or Somalia, as she passed northbound through the Suez Canal again just 11 days later. Apart from this, *Styliani's* voyages in the period included one into the Black Sea, and two from North Africa to Northern French ports and Rotterdam, probably with phosphate rock. From April 1938 she appears to have been inactive at Piraeus, but was reactivated in late 1939 for two voyages from the Mediterranean to the UK. *Styliani* was sunk by German air attack at Piraeus on 6th April 1941.

She was a fine old ship, completed in August 1896 by R. Thompson and Sons on the Wear as *Hillcrag,* and of 3,256gt. She was built for a single ship company, unimaginatively titled the Steamship Hillcrag Co. Ltd., but her interest lies in being one of relatively few deep-sea tramps owned in Liverpool, where her original manager was H. Evans and Co. This fleet was not large, although Evans did manage two ships for the Liverpool and Maranham Steamship Co. Ltd. Liverpool tramping fleets have not received the attention they deserve compared with the liner companies operating from the port, although her next Liverpool owner, John Herron and Co., was the subject of a three-part article by John MacRoberts in 'Sea Breezes' during 1974. This relates that *Hillcrag* was only Herron's second steamer, and he did not give it one of the 'Lord' names he favoured, although he registered her in the ownership of the Steamship Lord Lathom Co. Ltd.

Hillcrag was sold in 1908, and began a long and varied career under the Greek flag. Initially renamed *Orion,* she had five different owners/managers, before becoming *Patra* in 1932. In 1937 came her last change, to *Styliani* in the ownership of Aristides Pittas and C. Scrivanos of Piraeus. *[Courtesy Rick Cox]*

HAIN IN A HUNDRED

A BRITISH TRAMP FLEET AT WORK, NEW YEAR'S DAY 1900

Malcolm Cooper

The last two decades of the nineteenth century saw a massive increase in British steam tramp shipping. Surging coal exports to the industrialising world providing a dependable source of outward freight, while grain imports from the steppes of Russia, and the plains of North and South America provided an equally expanding inward cargo base. In addition, the development of triple-expansion engines made steamers competitive with sailing vessels on all but the longest bulk carrying trades, and British steam tramps found their way into the South Atlantic, the Indian Ocean and the Pacific in increasing numbers. This period of expansion saw the emergence of some very large tramp shipping companies. This article presents a snapshot of the operations of one of them at the beginning of the twentieth century.

Fleet growth and composition

The firm of Edward Hain and Son was in many ways a typical example of a large late Victorian tramp shipping company, although it retained some distinctive features which set it apart from other similar concerns. The Hain family had been ship owners in St Ives on the north Cornish coast since the early decades of the nineteenth century, but up until the late 1870s the business had been a small local concern, usually operating only two or three wooden schooners or brigantines, and not adding its first and only iron-hulled sailing vessel, the Hayle-built barquentine *T.S.B.*, until 1877. A year later, however, the family ordered its first steamer, the *Trewidden*, from John Readhead and Company of South Shields. The arrival of the *Trewidden* signalled the beginning of a spectacular period of expansion. No fewer than 17 new steamers were ordered in the 1880s, and another 17 in the 1890s, all from the same builder

that had produced the pioneer steamer. All were given Cornish names beginning with *Tre-* (place) and all were registered at the home port of St Ives, despite the fact that few if any of them would ever visit it.

Of the 35 nineteenth-century built steamers, eight had been sold (one as a constructive total loss, subsequently repaired and sold by the underwriters) and five lost by the end of the 1890s (the most recent the *Trevean*, stranded off St Nazaire on 14th November 1899 and only abandoned as unsalvageable in the last days of the year). Thus on 1st January 1900, the Hain fleet stood at 22 vessels. The oldest was the 1885-built *Treneglos*, the newest the *Trevessa*, which had only joined the fleet in October 1899. A comparison of these vessels demonstrates the extent to which the steam tramp had grown in size over the last decade and a half. The *Treneglos*, one of only two compound-engined vessels left in the fleet, was 81 feet shorter and roughly 10 feet narrower and shallower than the brand new *Trevessa*. As a result, the new vessel measured just over 3,500 tons gross compared to her older fleet mate's 1,560, and had well over double her carrying capacity.

Hain would not consolidate its fleet into a single limited company, the Hain Steamship Co. Ltd., until 1901. Prior to that, each vessel was run as a separate entity, some as single-ship limited companies (the *Trevessa*, for example, was owned by the Trevessa Steamship Co. Ltd.), and some (such as the *Treneglos*) along more traditional lines, with individual owners holding 64th shares directly. The parent firm of Edward Hain and Son managed all the vessels. In addition, the Hain family retained significant shareholdings in all the vessels and single-ship companies. The family patriarch, Edward Hain (III) had died on 1st July 1899, willing his shares to his wife Grace. The will had yet to settle at the end of the year, but the company itself was controlled by Edward the elder's son Edward Hain (IV), who had been the driving force behind the move to steam, and who would, in fact, remain in control of the business until it was sold to P&O during the First World War. The family together owned, for example, 27/64ths of the *Treneglos* and 43/64ths of the 1893-built *Trefusis*. The remaining shares were largely held by local Cornish investors, many of them with long business or personal connections with the Hain family, although in some cases Readhead the shipbuilder also held a minority stake.

The accident-prone *Trefusis* (2,642/1893). As well as the incidents described in the text, she ran aground on the Northumberland coast in 1902. But like so many ships of her generation, U-boat war finished her, and she was captured and sunk by bombs by *U 65* off Sardinia on 7th April 1917. *[J. & M. Clarkson]*

Shareholding was more diverse in the single-ship companies – indeed, one of the reasons why the Hains would have adopted such corporate structures for some of their vessels would have been to widen their investor base. The Trevessa Steamship Co. Ltd., incorporated only months before, was a typical example. It was capitalized at £37,000 – approximately the building cost of the *Trevessa* – split into 370 shares of £100 each. £100 was still a significant sum of money (equivalent to £5-10,000 today), but it was only a sixth of the cost of one share if the vessel had been sold to investors in 64th shares. The Hain family held 34 shares, the Readheads 16, and the Cornish trading company Thomas Bolitho and Sons (a long term supporter of the Hain shipping venture) 20. Most of the rest were held in ones and twos by individual investors, many of them St Ives based, including a number of active and retired master mariners. In total, the 370 shares were spread about 169 shareholders, the furthest flung being two of the company's agents in the Black Sea.

Fleet disposition

The shipping industry was no more likely to get a sailor home for a public holiday in 1900 than it is today. Only seven of Hain's 22 vessels were actually in port on New Year's Day, and only two of these, the *Tremayne* at Liverpool and the *Trelawny* at Belfast, were actually in the United Kingdom. The rest of the fleet was widely spread. This said, the Hain flag with the white initials E H on a red background was far from encompassing the seven seas. Apart from the two vessels in UK ports, the fleet was all to be found in a quadrilateral roughly defined by the Atlantic and Indian Oceans, encompassing the Mediterranean and Black Seas. No vessel was north of latitude 55 north, west of longitude 65 west, south of latitude 35 south or east of longitude 80 east. The outliers were the *Trelawny*, moored at Belfast, the *Trevilly*, moored at Rosario, the *Trewellard*, at Table Bay, and the *Trewidden* and *Trelyon*, each six days away from Colombo on passage from South Wales via the Suez Canal.

Opposite page: The *Trevessa* (3,566/1899) the last ship to join the fleet in the nineteenth century, remained with the company for twenty years. Sold to Chilean buyers in 1920 she was wrecked at Valparaiso in 1926. *[Ships in Focus]*

Left: The second *Trelyon* (3,099/1897) was carrying coal to Colombo at the date of this survey. She was to become one of Hain's war losses, mined off Scarborough in July 1917. *[J. & M. Clarkson collection]*

Ship	Built	Deployment on 1.1.1900
Treneglos	1885	Bilbao (arrived from La Pallice/sailed for Cardiff 11.1)
Tremayne	1886	Liverpool (arrived from Sulina/sailed for Cardiff 3.1)
Trelawny	1888	Belfast (arrived from Sulina/sailed for Barry 4.1)
Trewellard	1889	Table Bay (arrived from Cardiff/sailed for Buenos Aires 8.1)
Trevorian	1889	Mediterranean (passed Malta 31.12, Cardiff for Port Said)
Treglisson	1889	Biscay (sailed Penarth 30.12 for Port Said)
Trevalgan	1890	S Atlantic (sailed St Vincent, Cape Verde 27.12, Cardiff for Simonstown)
Trevaylor	1890	Port Said (arrived from Cardiff/sailed for Dunkirk 12.1)
Tregurno	1891	Mediterranean (passed Malta 2.1, Port Said for Penarth)
Trevanion	1891	S Atlantic (sailed Simonstown 30.12 for Rosario)
Trewidden	1891	Indian Ocean (to arrive Colombo 6.1 from Barry via Suez Canal)
Tregenna	1892	S Atlantic (sailed Dakar late 12, Cardiff for Buenos Aires)
Trefusis	1893	S Atlantic (to arrive Montevideo 3.1 from Madeira)
Trevelyan	1894	Mid-Atlantic (to arrive St Vincent, Cape Verde 3.1, Barry for Buenos Aires)
Trevethoe	1895	Aegean (to arrive Smyrna 2.1 from Penarth)
Trevarrack	1895	Black Sea (sailed Constantinople 28.12 for Theodossia)
Trevose	1896	St Vincent CV (arrived from Brindisi/sailed for Rosario 2.1)
Trevilley	1897	Rosario (arrived from St Vincent, Cape Verde /sailed for Buenos Aires 4.1)
Trelyon	1897	Indian Ocean (to arrive Colombo 6.1 from Barry via Suez Canal)
Trekieve	1898	Mid Atlantic (to arrive Gravesend 16.1 from Buenos Aires)
Tresillian	1899	S Atlantic (sailed from Buenos Aires 29.12 for London and Hamburg)
Trevessa	1899	Montevideo (arrived from Genoa 31.12/sailed for Bremen 5.1)

While the available sources do not give information on cargoes, the pattern of the company's trade is fairly clear. In common with most of the British tramp shipping industry, Hain vessels carried coal on most outward voyages. Indeed, all the company's ships that sailed from UK ports in the closing months of 1899 did so from South Wales coal ports. In most, if not all cases, the final homeward cargo would be grain or other bulk foodstuffs such as rice. Intermediate voyages, from the point of delivery of the coal cargo to the port where the grain or rice was to be loaded, were most likely made in ballast.

The Hain fleet was heavily deployed in the South American grain trade, with a total of 11 vessels either sailing to/from the River Plate or in one of its ports. The pull of the South Atlantic on the fleet was being further accentuated by the Boer War, with one vessel in Table Bay, another on her way there and one recently sailed to pick up a homeward cargo on the Plate. Apart from the two vessels carrying Welsh coal out to Colombo, both of which would subsequently go to Burmese rice ports to load for home, the remainder of the fleet was deployed in the Mediterranean and Black Sea trades. The smaller and older units of the fleet were, unsurprisingly, occupied in these shorter-distance trades – indeed only one of the six vessels built before 1890 was engaged in the southern hemisphere.

Mishaps

As already mentioned, the Hain fleet had suffered its last casualty in November 1899 when the *Trevean* stranded fatally outside St Nazaire. The two salvage vessels working the wreck had only concluded their task on 28th December, discharging

much of the coal cargo into lighters before leaving the vessel to break up. The new century was to start in a relatively trouble-free fashion – indeed Hain would not lose another ship to marine hazard until the *Trevorian* foundered in the Bay of Biscay in 1910 – but with a fleet of such size, it was inevitable that there were some mishaps.

The most serious casualty may already have taken place by New Year's Day. The *Trefusis* arrived at Montevideo on 3rd January in tow of the London tramp steamer *Min* having broken her propeller shaft somewhere in the South Atlantic. The vessel had carried coal from Cardiff to Madeira and was proceeding from the latter port to the Plate in ballast to load for home. She was moved from Montevideo to Buenos Aires by the tug *Huracan* on 5th January, presumably to repair, but her troubles did not end there. Two days later, while at anchor in the roads, the *Trefusis* dragged her anchors in a *pampero* and drifted down on the British cruiser *Pegasus*. The resulting collision appears to have damaged the tramp more severely, and she had to be dry-docked with several plates bent or broken and her fore-hold flooded.

The company's other January marine incident occurred in home waters. On the morning of 16th January, the *Trekieve*, bound from Buenos Aires for London and Bremen, collided with two Thames barges below Gravesend. Both vessels, the *Quail* of London with a cargo of bricks and the *Maidstone* of Rochester with coal, sank, but the two crews were rescued and the *Trekieve* herself proceeded apparently undamaged.

One other vessel was beset by mishap before the Hain fleet's first set of 20th century voyages was completed. The *Trevose* had arrived safely at Rosario on 22nd January

Trevorian (2,270/1889) foundered in the Bay of Biscay on 25th January 1910 whilst on a voyage from Barry Docks to Taranto with coal. *[J. & M. Clarkson]*

1900 got off to a bad start for *Trekieve* (3,087/1898). In January she was in collision with two Thames barges, both of which sank, in the river below Gravesend. *Trekieve* survived until April 1917 when torpedoed by *U 35* west of Gibraltar *[J. & M. Clarkson collection]*

Trevose (3,112/1896) was to be another U-boat victim, torpedoed by *U 81* in the Atlantic in March 1917 when outward bound with Tyne coal. *[J. & M. Clarkson]*.

The second *Trevanion* (2,437/1891) was commanded by Cornishman George Gyles in 1900. She was to be another sale to Greece, becoming *Michail* in 1911, and disappearing after leaving Cardiff in October 1916. *[J. & M. Clarkson]*

Trevaylor (2,426/1890) had perhaps the longest career of any Hain vessel from the nineteenth century. She was sold to Greek owners in 1911 as *Sifnos*, then went to Norway as *Hallingdal*, to Denmark as *Amleth* and later *Polaris*, finishing her tour of Scandinavia under the same name and the Swedish flag. She was broken up in 1956. *[J. & M. Clarkson]*.

Built and engined by John Readhead and Co. at South Shields, as were all of Hain's nineteenth century steamers, *Tremayne* (1,541/1886) was one of the few ships of the fleet in a home port, Liverpool, on 1st January 1900. She had a singularly long life: sold in 1905 she steamed on under the Swedish or Finnish flag as *Helios*, *Helny* and *Frigg* until she sank off Kiel in April 1944 at the age of 58 years. *[Roy Fenton collection]*

and had subsequently moved down to Buenos Aires to complete her cargo of linseed and cattle. While leaving the latter port, she struck the dock wall slightly and, while no damage was suspected at the time, she began to leak on her second day at sea. She put back to Montevideo on 23rd February with her fore-hold flooded and the cargo in it damaged. The Uruguayan authorities slapped her in quarantine, and she thus had to go to Buenos Aires. Here, in addition to the removal of the damaged grain, the authorities insisted on the total discharge of her livestock, while docking revealed that the damage was more extensive than first suspected, necessitating the removal of even more hold cargo. It was 17th March before she was ready to sail, but even then the beleaguered master did not enjoy a trouble-free passage home. On 11th April the *Trekieve* was reported as having put into St Vincent in the Cape Verde Islands short of coal due to bad weather, and on the 21st of the same month, she reported the loss of 71 of her deck cargo of cattle, apparently due to foot and mouth disease. When the *Trekieve* finally reached Gravesend on 26 April, the total loss had gone up to 88 bullocks and 8 sheep – apparent proof that the inconvenient Uruguayan quarantine had been justified.

Masters and crews

While the Hain fleet might be sailing across half the oceans of the world, and its ships never call at the home port of St Ives, its officers were almost as solidly West Country as its managers and shareholders. Of the 22 men in command on 1st January 1900, only two, one Londoner and one Welshman, had been born outside of Cornwall or Devon. No fewer than nine masters hailed from St Ives itself, including two members of the Hain family. As might be expected, the masters were solidly middle-aged. Most were in their 40s or early 50s – only one was aged under 38, and only one aged over 53. It is striking that the four masters aged over 50 were all Cornishmen, three of them natives of St Ives. All were long-term servants of a company which, despite its size and range of operations, was still very much a local family business. George Gyles, the 51 year old master of the *Trevanion*, was a typical example. Born in St Ives in 1848, he had earned his master's certificate at Bristol in 1874 and had moved from sail to steam in 1877. He had entered Hain service as a first officer in mid-1889 but had been granted his first command later the same year. The *Trevanion*, which he joined in 1897, was his fourth Hain command, and he would stay with her until 1905. He then commanded a further three company vessels before retiring in 1914 at the age of 65.

In 1900, Hain ships were only carrying two deck officers in addition to the master. These were almost as heavily West Country as the men who commanded them – 19 of the first mates were from Cornwall or Devon, and 12 of the second mates. All but one of the steamers carried three engineers (the *Treneglos* had only two). Here, the West Country dominance was less strong, but still marked – 14 chief engineers, six second engineers and eight third engineers. There were actually three vessels in which all six officers were West Countrymen. Most officers who did not hail from Cornwall or Devon came from elsewhere in Britain, the only exceptions being the second engineer of the *Trevalgan*, who was a Swede, and the chief and second engineers of the *Trevanion*, who, rather unusually, were both Greek.

Officers tended to be long-term company employees who remained aboard the same vessel for repeat voyages.

Ship	Master	Age	Born
Treneglos	E J Couch	38	Plymouth
Tremayne	John Jones	47	Aberporth
Trelawny	E C Strike	38	Porthleven
Trewellard	Samuel Gorley	43	Brixham
Trevorian	Samuel Gregory	52	Haytor
Treglisson	Joseph Blackie	47	Woolwich
Trevalgan	William Stevens	53	St Ives
Trevaylor	Thomas Williams	38	Falmouth
Tregurno	Thomas Daniel	63	St Ives
Trevanion	George Gyles	51	St Ives
Trewidden	J Hodges	53	St Ives
Tregenna	G Shepherd	48	Mullion
Trefusis	Edward Hain	38	St Ives
Trevelyan	James Sincock	40	St Ives
Trevethoe	F Robbins	43	Devon
Trevarrack	John Hain	42	St Ives
Trevose	W S Roach	43	St Ives
Trevilley	James Hendy	44	Porthleven
Trelyon	Charles Blake	41	Brixham
Trekieve	E F Roach	36	St Ives
Tresillian	John D Luke	47	Cornwall
Trevessa	Joseph Quiller	45	Plymouth

This was not the case with the remainder of the crew, who were signed on and discharged on a voyage-by-voyage basis, and had little reason or opportunity to develop ship or company loyalties. As a result of this, seamen, firemen and even the warrant officers were a far more polyglot bunch than their leaders.

The crew of the *Trevaylor*, signed on at Cardiff on 8th December 1899 for her voyage to Port Said, was fairly typical. Apart from Captain Williams, the two mates (one a West Countryman and one a Geordie) and the three engineers (from Newcastle, Cardiff and Bristol), the crew totalled a bosun, donkeyman, steward, cook, mess deck steward, six deckhands and five firemen. The bosun, donkeyman and one of the ABs were Scots, the Steward and another of the ABs were Cornish, and the 17-year old mess deck steward (on his first voyage) was from the Tyne. The cook was a Dane, and of the remaining four deckhands, two were Italian, one an American and one simply gave his place of birth as Africa. The firemen were made up of two Germans, an Irishman, a Maltese and a native of Gibraltar. The chief engineer, the bosun and the donkeyman were all in their early 50s; of the rest of the crew, only one was aged over 40 and the average age of all 22 aboard was $31\frac{1}{2}$, which was fairly close to the norm for the fleet as a whole. Apart from the officers, only the steward, the donkeyman and two of the deckhands had served on the *Trevaylor* on her previous voyage, although four others had been on other

Hain vessels. There would be no desertions and the whole crew was discharged intact at Cardiff on 12th February. It had been a fairly short voyage, and there were presumably few reasons to desert in Port Said or Alexandria, which were the ship's only foreign ports of call, but rates of desertion were fairly low across the fleet – far lower than was the case on the long haul voyages of deepwater sailing ships, on which it was not uncommon for nobody but the officers and apprentices to be left aboard after a few days in an Australian or American Pacific coast port.

Just as the Hain family operated its ships for profit, so did its crews work for wages. The firemen aboard the *Trevaylor* were paid £4 a month and the deckhands £3.15.0.

The wages of the warrant officers ranged between £4.10.0. for the bosun and £6 for the steward (although the young mess deck steward was paid only £2). The master's wages were not (as was usual) shown on the crew agreement, but what is interesting about the rest is that the engineers were significantly better paid than the deck officers. The three engineers were paid £16, £10.10.0 and £7 respectively – the first mate was paid £9.10.0, less than the second engineer, and the second mate £7, the same as the third engineer. This was a common pattern across the fleet, and a reminder that the most important man aboard a steam tramp after the captain was the one entrusted with keeping the engines running.

Opposite upper: *Tregurno* (2,432/1891) was in the Mediterranean at the beginning of 1900, and was to continue her career with owners in that area. From 1911 she ran as the Greek *Pandelis*, although the British Shipping Controller took her over between 1918 and 1920. Taking the name *Hellas* in 1934 she was broken up in Italy later that year. *[J. & M. Clarkson]*
Opposite lower: *Trevethoe* (2,097/1895) became the Norwegian *Erviken* in 1911, but her neutrality during the First World War proved no protection against submarine attack, and she was sunk by *U 64* off the Spanish coast whilst on a voyage from San Reggio to Seville. *[J. & M. Clarkson]*
This page top: *Trewidden* (2,613/1891) went to Glasgow owners as *Gartland* in 1915. In January 1918 she was torpedoed off the Owers Light by *UB 30*. *[J. & M. Clarkson]*.
Middle: A Swedish owner took *Trevarrack* (2,098/1895) when Hain sold her in 1914, and as *Iris* she was wrecked off the Essex coast on Christmas Day 1917. *[J. & M. Clarkson]*
Bottom: *Trevelyan* (3,066/1894) was a U-boat victim which just survived. She was so badly damaged by a torpedo off the French coast in December 1917 that she was declared a constructive total loss, but such was the demand for ships that she was sold to Italians and reconditioned at Cherbourg to emerge as *Esperia* in 1919. It was a short reprieve, however, as she was broken up at Genoa in 1924. *[J. & M. Clarkson]*.

TRAMPING INTO OBSCURITY
Steam's Indian summer on the Thames: Part 1
Roy Fenton

The total number of British ship owners must run into the tens of thousands. Tracing the history of one is often difficult, as records were almost invariably destroyed once trading ceased. The maritime historian unwillingly accepts that the majority of ship owners are going to remain obscure, but still has a desire to record something of their life and times. Articles in this occasional series will set down what is known about loose groupings of owners of deep sea or coastal tramp steamers for whom it is unlikely that enough information will ever emerge to write a full history. Of course, if any of these jottings stimulate readers to reveal their knowledge of an organisation featured, then the author would be delighted to hear from them in order for a fuller account to be compiled and published.

Coastal steam's Indian summer

The British steam coaster was perfected by 1890. A compact vessel had been developed which, with a length of around 150 feet and a shallow draft, could trade profitably to a wide variety of ports. A two-cylinder compound or more rarely a triple-expansion engine propelled it at an economical nine knots, which was quite adequate given the modest lengths of the voyages and the nature of the bulk cargoes carried, which were rarely time-sensitive. It is some measure of the success of its design that, half a century on from its zenith, the steam coaster enjoyed something of a renaissance.

Following an unprecedentedly long depression in shipping, the late 1930s saw a modest revival in freight rates. Optimistic coastal ship owners went ahead and ordered new ships, usually but not always expensive motor ships. Others were more cautious, and bought ageing and therefore cheap steam coasters calculating that, in the event of a renewed slump, their financial exposure would be small. The situation at the end of the Second World War added impetus, with cargoes a-plenty but ships in short supply. The industry had not forgotten the lesson of the 1920s, that the post-war boom in freight rates could well be short-lived and followed by a desperate depression, and some new and some existing owners put their trust in superannuated steamers. The best known exponent of the practice of running old coasters was Thomas Kettlewell and Sons of Hull whose Holderness Steamship Co. Ltd. had the biggest and longest-lived fleet of super-annuated steamers on the UK coast in post-war years. But most of these new-found owners of elderly coasters were based on the Thames, possibly because in London there was a community of shipbrokers and agents who were acutely aware of the opportunities during a bull market for ships. This article explores the London owners who took part in this brief renaissance of steam coaster owning, in a period roughly from the mid 1930s to 1955, drawing its information – in the absence of other sources - largely from the histories of the companies' various vessels.

Frederick G. Browne

Frederick G. Browne became a ship owner in 1939, acquiring the Canadian-built First World War standard *Widestone* (3,192/1920), whose management was entrusted to Turnbull, Scott and Co. *Widestone* was torpedoed in the North Atlantic in November 1942, tragically with the loss of all the 42 crew and gunners aboard. It is likely that Fredericke Browne used the war risk insurance money from *Widestone* to fund a fleet of smaller vessels intended for east coast trades and which were managed by Anthony and Bainbridge Ltd. of Newcastle-upon-Tyne

First of these purchased by Browne in March 1943 was the 180-foot *Guelder Rose* (700/1913). She was unusual in being Dutch built, like her sister *Blush Rose* illustrated in 'Record' 30. *Guelder Rose* had been through two short ownerships since leaving the Richard Hughes fleet in 1941, but was destined to be Browne's longest serving ship.

Guelder Rose, seen in Richard Hughes ownership, became *Riversider* in 1947 and was sold to Connell and Grace Ltd. of Newcastle in 1951 as *Akenside*. She was broken up in 1954. *[National Waterfront Museum 358/656]*

In August 1943, Browne added the *Kilrea* (767/1911), built in Dundee for London coal merchants, but since owned on the Tees, Mersey, Clyde and in Belfast. *Kilrea* sank in February 1944 following a collision with a tug near Flamborough Head whilst on a voyage from Aberdeen to Ridham Dock with wood pulp. *Quaysider* (595/1913) was the next acquisition, bought in partnership with an Albert Furst in November 1944. About this time, these partners acquired their biggest ship, the east coast collier *Spanker* (1,875/1917) which had been built in Sunderland for Witherington and Everett of Newcastle-upon-Tyne. The name of *Quaysider* was to inspire a naming scheme for this small fleet, and in 1947 the *Guelder Rose* was renamed *Riversider* whilst *Spanker* became *Hillsider*. The partnership with Furst was dissolved in 1947, and Browne moved from London to St. Helier, Jersey. Perhaps retired, he was unable or unwilling to acquire further ships, and *Quaysider* was sold in 1949, *Hillsider* in 1950 and *Riversider* in 1951, all for further trading.

Challis, Stern and Co. Ltd.

This small fleet specialised in coasters at the lower end of the size scale bought right at the end of their lives: none was to trade for a further owner. However, they did institute a corporate naming scheme. Acquisitions began in May 1940 with the *Norbritt* (287/1917), a 120-foot steamer built for Joseph Monks and Co. Ltd., Warrington to run in local trades out of the Mersey. Coincidentally, the next purchase, *Foamville* (403/1916) came in 1942 from a company set up by the sons of Joseph Monks, John S. Monks and Co. Ltd. of Liverpool. By

May 1944 Challis, Stern had floated the Warren Shipping Co. Ltd. which acted as managers for the next addition, another former west coast steamer, *Edern* (466/1920), the largest in this modest fleet at 152 feet. In 1946 'Warren' names were adopted across the fleet, *Norbritt* becoming *Warren Court*, *Foamville* being renamed *Warren Field*, and *Edern* becoming *Warren Chase*.

Above: *Warren Court* (1) had already carried the names *Lillena*, *Madame Lundi*, *Whitgift*, *Robrix* and *Norbritt*. She was broken up at Gateshead in 1953. *[Roy Fenton collection]*
Left: *Warren Chase* had a simpler history, having been *Edern* until 1946. She too was demolished at Gateshead, in 1954. *[J. and M. Clarkson]*

Warren Field was bought by Challis, Stern in 1942 and renamed in 1946, ending up in 1953 with breakers C.W. Dorkin and Co. Ltd. at Gateshead who demolished many steam coasters. Her list of former owners was long, and as *Polly Bridge* she was owned in Hull, Swansea, Sunderland, Burry Port, and Cardiff over just eight years. From 1924 she was Monks *Foamville*. *[Fotoflite incorporating Skyfotos]*

In March 1947 came *Snowcrete* (351/1921) which was renamed *Warren Grove*, her former name harking back to ownership by a cement manufacturer in the late 1920s. She was short-lived: on 9th November 1948 she sank after developing a leak in heavy weather north east of Arbroath whilst on a voyage from Hartlepool to Buckie with coal. Tragically, only three of the crew were rescued.

There was now a five-year gap before the small *Graham F* (294/1920) joined the fleet in 1953, this time being owned by Warren Shipping Co. Ltd. and renamed *Warren Court* (2). Since 1948 she had belonged to an even more minor London owner, the one-ship Falconer Coasters Ltd. The other ships were then transferred to the ownership of Warren Shipping Co. Ltd. The three earlier ships were sold to breakers in 1953 and 1954, leaving the second *Warren Court* to sail on alone until 1957.

The managers of these small coasters were an Arthur Jackson and an Ernest Scott. The only clues to who were Challis, Stern and Co. Ltd. are the name on a series of labels for rum bottles, and that this company was registered in 1925,

being listed as shipping agents in pre-Second World War directories.

Culliford and Clark Ltd.

Culliford Shipping Ltd. began in December 1937 with moderate-sized ships and generally down-sized to coasters. The management company, Culliford and Clark Ltd., were ship brokers and briefly managed the Spanish steamer *Deva* (2,153/1907). The first ship owned, the Norwegian-built *Hester* (1,199/1907), was scuttled in damaged condition at Rochefort on 18th June 1940 during the battle for France and although refloated was not repaired. By then the management company had taken on three interesting steamers built for the timber trade, the *Highwear* (1,173/1936), *Highwave* (1,178/1936) and *Highwood* (1,177/1936) owned by the bizarrely-named High Hook Shipping Co. Ltd. Conventional if aged coasters then arrived, *Montalto* (623/1902), *Corrib* (624/1902), *Dicky* (501/1901), *Fleswick* (647/1899), *Glen Tilt* (871/1920 and previously the delightfully-named *Goodwill of Bristol*), the Dutch *Helmond* (983/1921) and *Haarlem* (970/1917). There were several

Graham F was bought from Falconer Coasters Ltd. by Challis, Stern and Co. Ltd. in 1953 and renamed *Warren Court* (2). Until 1948 she had been *Lady Thomas*, owned by a Liverpool company. *Warren Court* was broken up in Belgium during 1957. *[World Ship Society Ltd.]*

A number of former Kelly colliers spent some of their last years in the ownership of London companies, including *Montalto*. She had been built by Ailsa as *The Princess* for John Hay and Sons, Glasgow, passing to Kelly subsidiary William Barkley and Co. Ltd. in 1929 to become *Montalto*. Culliford bought her in August 1940, but lost her just eight months later. *[J. & M. Clarkson]*

casualties. *Highwave* was bombed and sunk off the Kentish Knock Light Vessel on 30th January 1940 whilst taking a cargo of coal from Hull to Lorient. *Montalto* was bombed and sunk at Rochester on 17th April 1941 having arrived from Ipswich to load cement. Although raised she was later broken up. *Glen Tilt* was torpedoed and sunk by an E-boat off Lowestoft on 12th December 1942 whilst carrying cement from London to Middlesbrough. Management of the two surviving High Hook ships ceased in 1946. Others were sold, the last coaster *Dicky* going in 1948 leaving just the larger US-built *Granton Glen* (2,485/1918) to be taken over later that year, along with any other assets of the company, by Evan, Thomas Radcliffe of Cardiff.

An interesting sideline was trawler management, Culliford and Clark Ltd. managing the *Somersby* (272/1918)

and *Margaret Rose* (348/1912). Culliford Associated Lines Ltd. registered in 1941 had the Fleetwood fishing magnate Basil Parkes as a director, but rather than trawlers owned the former Canadian-based steamer *Sagona* (808/1912) and managed the ex-Dutch coaster *Gertruda* (137/127). Who might Culliford and Clark have been is something of a mystery, as by 1948 the eminence grise was a Frederick Thompson, who owned all but a handful of the shares in the Culliford Shipping Co. Ltd.

Culliford and Clark had a pleasing funnel design: black basic with a white band on which there was a large red diamond. On the red was a smaller white diamond with to either side a white letter C, the letter to the left being reversed so that the design was symmetrical.

In 1936 three large coasters were built by Short Brothers Ltd., Sunderland for the Springwell Shipping Co. Ltd., London. As the very high set derricks suggest, they were intended to work in the timber trade. They quickly passed to the High Hook Shipping Co. Ltd., and in 1939 this came under the management of Frederick Thompson, the man behind Culliford Shipping Co. Ltd. *Highwood*, seen here, became *Spanker* in January 1954, but in August of that year was wrecked at the entrance to the New Waterway. *[Fotoflite incorporating Skyfotos]*

George W. Grace

George William Grace had a long pedigree as a shipowner. He was a partner in the Newcastle-based Connell and Grace Ltd. established in 1914, his partner George Connell maintaining the Tyneside end with Grace based in London. Colours were similar: Grace used a black funnel with a green band edged with white, and a green flag carrying a white outline oblong. The Connell and Grace colours had a white 'C & G' on the green funnel band and also inside the oblong on the flag.

First evidence of independent operation was when Grace bought the *Pengam* (825/1918) in 1930. She had been the 'Kil' class patrol sloop HMS *Kildwick*, completed almost too late for the First World War, then converted into a rather unsatisfactory steam coaster. *Pengam* was quickly sold to Latvian owners and, renamed *Curonia*, continued to be managed by Grace for a year or two. Connell and Grace used a similar naming scheme for other ships they operated under the Latvian flag. Grace's next ship, the ocean-going *Roehampton* (4,163/1913), followed the same fast track to the same Riga owners. Originally the Cardiff-owned *Helmsloch*, she had stranded in the Straits of Messina in April 1934 under the intermediate name *Michael L*, and was bought by Grace

from the repairers. Management of *Roehampton* continued until her sale in 1940 (she served for part of the war under the Swiss flag as *Calanda*), but by then Grace had embarked on a coaster-buying spree.

In approximate order of acquisition from 1940 to 1942 came *Quickthorn* (409/1903), *Southport* (572/1914), *Southwick* (443/1917), *East Anglian* (870/1917), *Westown* (710/1921), *Monkstone* (867/1923), *Croham* (391/1921) and *Moray Firth* (541/1927). Two were to become losses, but due to marine rather than war causes. *Quickthorn* foundered in January 1942 off Skokholm whilst carrying coal from Newport to Londonderry and *Moray Firth* sank after a collision off Portknockie in March 1943 taking cement from London to Kirkwall. Others were quickly sold on, but in 1946 came another surge of acquisitions, more or less coinciding with the adoption of limited liability status as George W. Grace and Co. Ltd. With the war ended, so had restrictions on renamings, and the *Welsh Rose* (581/1922) entered the fleet as *Sussex Birch*. The two survivors from the wartime fleet were also renamed in like style, *Monkstone* becoming the first *Sussex Elm*, *East Anglian* becoming the *Sussex Oak*. In 1948 came the ageing *Porthmorna* (596/1910) to become *Sussex Ash*.

Another of Richard Hughes former fleet to join the ranks of London-based coaster operators in later years was the Goole-built *Welsh Rose* of 1922. Unusually, she had not been built for Hughes, but for Thomas Rose of Sunderland as *Brookside*, joining the Hughes fleet in its ill-judged expansion in 1929. The fleet survived receivership in 1937, but under new management the ships were gradually sold off as acceptable offers were received. *Welsh Rose* came to

George W. Grace and Co. Ltd. in May 1945 for a reported £13,000, prices clearly being inflated during the war, as she was now 23 years old. When wartime restrictions on renamings were lifted she became *Sussex Birch*, as seen here. Interestingly, she has not lost her mizzen mast, a feature which was often removed from coasters during the war as it restricted the arc of fire of the anti-aircraft guns often mounted on the superstructure aft. In this view, the crew of the

unladen *Sussex Birch* have left some of the hatch boards off, evidently anticipating good weather or a short voyage up Channel.

In July 1953, Sussex Birch found yet another owner, the Holderness Steamship Co. Ltd. of Hull, which squeezed another two and a half years service from her as *Holdernile*. She was broken up at Gateshead in November 1955.
[Fotoflite incorporating Skyfotos]

Above: the *Sussex Oak* had originally been the *Suffolk Coast* of a Coast Lines Ltd. predecessor, and when completed in May 1917 was employed as a Q-ship. The substantial masts and double derricks are reminders of her days in the regular liner trade, although the unusual crow's nest on her mainmast is a later addition. Sold by Coast Lines in 1938 she briefly became Monroe's *Kylebank*, and then *East Anglian* of Consolidated Fisheries Ltd of Grimsby. Bought by Grace in 1940, she could not be renamed

Sussex Oak until 1946. She too went to the Holderness Steamship Co. Ltd. in January 1954, but she was probably in too poor a condition even for them, as she went to breakers at Gateshead within six weeks. *[Fotoflite incorporating Skyfotos]*

Below: the *Sussex Ash* was 38 years old when Grace bought her in February 1948, by a short head the oldest ship he acquired. She had started life at Scotts of Bowling as *Onyx* for William Robertson of

Glasgow. She left his 'Gem Line' fleet in 1937 to become *Porthmorna* of what became the largest Cardiff-based coaster company, Richard P. Care and Co. Ltd. Perhaps not surprisingly given her age, *Sussex Ash* was the only one of Grace's ships to go direct to a breaker, Clayton and Davie Ltd. claiming her at Dunston-on-Tyne in April 1952. The timber deck cargo in this view might just suggest an origin for the tree names employed by the fleet. *[Fotoflite incorporating Skyfotos]*

The very last acquisition was almost calculated to make life difficult for future maritime historians and photo collectors. With the first *Sussex Elm* (ex-*Monkstone*) sold in 1951, the name was given to another almost identical coaster which had also carried the name *Monkstone*, indeed built at the same Bideford yard of the Hansen Shipbuilding and Ship Repairing Co. Ltd. (see 'Record' 14). The second *Sussex Elm* (873/1921) lasted just two years, rendering the company extinct when she was sold along with *Sussex Birch* in 1953, the fleet being marginally outlasted by that of Connell and Grace Ltd. which expired in 1954. Remarkably the latter pair, along with almost all of Grace's ageing steamers, found other owners, in four cases with the Hull-based fleet of the Holderness Steamship Co. Ltd. Only one of Grace's ships, the *Sussex Ash*, was sold directly to a shipbreaker, suggesting that, with its own house flag and naming scheme, the Grace operation took pride in its fleet and looked after its ships. *[To be concluded]*

The two *Sussex Elms* were virtually sisters, and to add to the confusion were both originally named *Monkstone* by their Bideford builders. The 1923 example (above) was bought first, coming in 1941 from Stone and Rolfe Ltd. of Llanelly who had taken *Monkstone* over without change of name in 1924. She was renamed *Sussex Elm* (1) in 1946. When sold in 1951, the Bristol Steam Navigation Co. Ltd. took her as *Sappho*, and she ended up with Comben Longstaff as *Kentbrook*, only to be wrecked off Orfordness in February 1954. *[Fotoflite incorporating Skyfotos]*

The second *Sussex Elm* (below) was completed in 1921 and quickly sold to Richard Hughes and Co. as *Wild Rose*. George Grace and Co. Ltd. bought and renamed her in 1951, only to sell her to the almost inevitable Holderness Steamship Co. Ltd. in 1953. As *Holdernene* she steamed on until 1958 when demolished in Dublin. The differences between the two sisters are subtle, and come down to such details as the top of the mainmasts (both have a distinct forward rake), the wheelhouse, the location of the stove pipes on the superstructure aft, and the vent immediately abaft the bridge. *[J. and M. Clarkson]*

PUTTING THE RECORD STRAIGHT

Letters, additions, amendments and photographs relating to articles in *any* issues of 'Record' are welcomed. Letters may be edited. Communications by e-mail are welcome, but senders are asked to include their postal address.

City sins

Tony Smythe, David Hodge and others have pointed out that the top photo on page 2 of 'Record' 33 is clearly the Chicago City *of 1892 and not the* Wells City, *as captioned. Paul Boot notes that the fleet list entry for* Bristol City *(5) is incorrect in claiming she was scrapped almost immediately after her sale in 1970. In fact, she continued on with owners Gemini Companhia Naviera S.A. of Panama, managed by Christos Lemos Sons and Co. Ltd. under the Greek flag as* Agelos Gabriel. *She was laid up at Chalkis on 17th June 1977, and after sale to Brodospas arrived at Split for demolition on 3rd April 1980.*

The Strait and Narrows

In 'Record' 32 page 216 along with the picture of the *Sutherland Grange* transiting a narrow passage is the author's quest for the correct location of the photograph. While on a cruise through this area last fall on the *Polar Star*, the ship passed through this same narrows. We too were able to get off the ship and photograph her as she transited the narrows. It is called Kirke Narrows and is in Monatanas Fjord, which is a considerable distance north of the Straits of Magellan. We passed through there on 18th November but did not get to the Straits of Magellan until the 21st.
HUBERT HALL, PO Box 476, Yarmouth, Nova Scotia B5A 4B4

Osbon observations

George Osbon must have travelled further north for his holidays as the shot of *Lancashire Coast* on page 29 of 'Record' 33 shows her leaving Aberdeen. The Torry Battery can be seen right with south inner breakwater light, the two Nissen huts behind her stern are now HMS *Scylla*, the headquarters of the Aberdeen Sea Cadets.
JIM POTTINGER, 1 Jesmond Circle, Aberdeen

The negative of *Queen of the Channel* has been printed in reverse. *Cymric* was broken up in October 1975, not 1957. *Savannah* is at Berth 101 at Southampton. The gentleman on page 22 is Westby Percival-Prescott.
BOB TODD and DAVID HODGE, National Maritime Museum, Greenwich, London SE10 9NF

Describing the choice of the name *Preston* as being unusual and random is misleading ('Record' 33, page 24). *Preston* was named after Robert Ropner's home, Preston Hall, near Stockton-on-Tees, which was given to the people and turned into a museum (Preston Park).
A.D. FROST, 32 Oakfield Close, Sunderland, Tyne and Wear SR3 3RT

Regfos ('Record' 33, page 23) was one of two cargo vessels owned by the Tyne and Wear Shipping Co. Ltd. of Newcastle, registered in 1926, with a separate company, France, Fenwick Tyne and Wear Co. Ltd., amongst the shareholders. The company had been formed in Sunderland in 1918 out of an earlier association between Fenwick, Stobart and Co. of London and Taylor, Sanderson, of Sunderland, to look after the chartering and agency work of the collier fleets which they each operated. Initially Taylor and Sanderson produced the greater amount of business in the joint enterprise but, as their influence declined, the 1918 company was formed by Wm. France, Fenwick who in 1901 had absorbed Fenwick, Stobart, and now held a controlling interest in the new company. Taylor and Sanderson also owned tugs on the Wear and these eventually passed to France, Fenwick Tyne and Wear Co. Ltd. and - with various later acquisitions - formed the basis of the company which eventually took on all towage on Tyne and Wear and which provides a direct link to the present North East coast towage services.

Tyne and Wear Shipping's other sea-going ship was the smaller, engines aft collier *Efos*, built at Ardrossan in 1924 and, unusually perhaps, engined by Plenty. Unlike her consort she was an early war loss. The names of the two vessels do not relate to some exotic fuel, however. The company had been set up in association with a firm of London coal factors: E. Foster and Co, and *Efos* was that company's telegraphic address. When *Regfos* was acquired her name was derived from *Reg*inald *Fos*ter, a principal of the Foster company. Two members of the Foster family were shareholders in Tyne and Wear Shipping.

Additional information is available in MacRae and Waine's 'Steam Collier Fleets' pages 57, 137 and 138, the France Fenwick official history of 1954, 'Fairplay' year books, and John Proud's '150 years of the Maltese Cross'.
JOHN LINGWOOD, 52 Nursery Road, Sunderland SR3 1NT
Thanks also to Charles Waine and A.D. Frost for confirming the origin of these names.

Agelos Gabriel, the former *Bristol City* (5). *[Paul Boot collection]*

Efos (see letter from John Lingwood) had an interesting history, having been built at Ardrossan as *Forestrow* (1,559/1924), seen above, sixth and last ship in a bold project by coaster-owners Mann, Macneal and Co. Ltd. of Glasgow to enter the market for larger colliers. Ownership was in the hands of the Forest Shipping Co. Ltd. but this venture quickly failed, precipitating the old-established Scottish coasting company into bankruptcy. *Forestrow* was bought by Tyne and Wear in 1927and renamed *Efos*. She sank on 26th February 1940 after striking what is described as a 'submerged object' four miles off Haisbro' Light Vessel whilst on a voyage from Sunderland to Devonport with a cargo of coal. *[J. and M. Clarkson]*

Notes from Eastern Scotland

On page 32 of 'Record' 25 you have a photograph of the *Philippe L.D* (the precise nomenclature – the caption misses the full-stop which those ships always had between the two final initials) and another after her conversion as the drill ship *Dalkeith*. It may seem strange that she had no less than four names under Salvesen ownership in the space of only two years. I was working for the company at the time, and gave slight assistance to Graeme Somner in his masterly book on the company's ships, published in 1984 as 'From 70 North to 70 South'. Indeed, the explanation of the names was one of the few parts which emanated from me rather than Graeme.

At that time, Salvesen already had one drill ship named *Dalmahoy*, after a small village to the west of Edinburgh with a championship golf course, close to which one of the Salvesens lived. The company decided to purchase a second ship for conversion to a drill ship and continuing the golf course theme it was decided to name her *Gullane*, a slightly larger village to the east of Edinburgh which has a number of famous golf courses (including the championship course at Muirfield). It soon became clear that the pronunciation of the name – which Edinburgh people usually call 'Ghillon' – was causing problems (I remember one foreigner interested in chartering the ship calling her 'Joolani') so it was decided to use the *Dal* prefix of the first ship as the continuing naming system and she was renamed *Dalkeith* after a town south of Edinburgh.

Having identified the ship as suitable for conversion, there was inevitably a delay while detailed designs were made, the conversion contract was investigated, and the finances were put in place. It was decided that the ship would be traded on the short-term charter market for iron ore cargoes but that she should not carry a name associated with the drill ship operations. For the best part of a year, during which she carried several ore cargoes to ports such as Bidston, she was given the traditional Salvesen cargo ship name of *Soutra*, named after a hill south of Edinburgh, which conformed to the pattern of having a name beginning with the first letter of the owning company's name and ending with the second (S-----a).

As if three names were not enough, when the conversion of the ship was nearing completion, Salvesen fixed her on a two-year time-charter to a company who wanted to use their own name for the duration of the charter – so she became the *Wingate*, her fifth name in only just over two years!

On page 235 of 'Record 32' I was interested in the two photographs of those war-built engines-aft motor ships. The *Serene Med* and a number of other ships in the Hellenic Med Line of Petropoulos were regular callers at Granton and Methil in the 1960s with cargoes of esparto grass from North Africa. His fleet was rather a motley collection and the CI-M-AV1s were among the largest ships to be employed on that trade with any regularity. His ships flew a variety of flags: some were Greek, others were among the first to fly the flag of the newly-independent Cyprus, one or two flew the Lebanese flag. Sometimes his ships carried full cargoes of grass, but on other occasions the grass was a deck-cargo (or also in the upper 'tween decks) with general cargo for discharge elsewhere in the lower 'tween decks. I assumed that there was an association with Euxine in terms of attracting cargo for their outward-bound non-conference cargo lines; Euxine didn't normally carry general cargo homebound whereas Hellenic Med did.

P.G. Callimanopoulos' Hellenic Lines, despite the similarity of name, was a different outfit to Hellenic Med. Their ships appeared on the esparto grass run only occasionally but the *Egyptos* came at least once. These ships were normally much smarter than Hellenic Med's tonnage. When the CI-M-AV1s called with a full cargo, it took several days to discharge them as they could carry a rather higher tonnage than the average tramp ship in this unpopular trade.

COLIN MENZIES, 17 Bickenhall Mansions, London W1U 6BP

Gordon Castle

I don't think you have yet mentioned the identification of the mystery ship photo on page 49 of 'Record' 25. I am quite confident that it is the *Gordon Castle* and I know that Malcolm Cooper shares this view.

IAN FARQUHAR, RD2, Dunedin, New Zealand

Essex error
I was interested to see Laurence Dunn's photograph of
Essex Abbey (4,331/1907) on page 220 of 'Record' 32. She is
not the same ship of the name (3,595/1911) on page 174 of
'Record' 31. The younger ship was earlier in the fleet. I saw
the ship in Laurence's view across the harbour from Fowey
at the mouth of Pont Pill about 1933. I have a poor photo of
Loyal Devonian at Waterford which confirms the layout of
the *Essex Abbey* of 1911, particularly sampson posts at the
break of poop.
IVOR ROOKE, 'Spinnakers', Chalkdock Lane, Itchenor,
Chichester, West Sussex PO20 7DE

Piecing together the *Meccano* story
The *Meccano* ('Record' 33) was Denny's yard number 1071
and was described as a twin screw creek steamer-type
experimental vessel for the builders. Although delivered
without a proper superstructure, Denny's general
arrangement plan in the 'Denny List' shows her as she
would have appeared had she entered service, with the
typical open flying deck running from stem to stern and a
tall funnel typical of the creek steamers built for such
undertakings as the Irrawaddy Flotilla Company.
    On the face of it, the vane wheel concept would
appear to be a quite inefficient method of propulsion, with
the vanes acting only partially in the water and producing
much spray. In fact, the trials figures quoted by Denny
show a surprising result.

	Displacement	Speed	IHP	RPM
Geared vane wheels	183 tons	10.3 kts	348	71
Ordinary screws	183 tons	10.2 kts	384	272

Vane wheels produced a slightly greater speed on a reduced
horsepower, which I would not have expected.
    Dennys went on to build another eight vessels of
this type. The 'Denny List' states that, regarding the
second vessel, the *Fano* of 1924, 'the experiment of fitting a
creek steamer with vane wheels was a qualified failure'. She
was unable to tow a sampan astern due to the wash and
when she stopped to pick up passengers in the stream she
was very difficult to control in anything of a breeze, due to
the rudders being placed ahead of the wheels. Severe
vibration was also felt. The *Fano* was converted to a
conventional twin-screw ship two years after entering
service. However, subsequent vessels appeared to be more
successful, with modifications such as triple rudders instead
of twin, and setting up the wheels so that opposite vanes
did not enter the water simultaneously to reduce vibration.
    As to the name, Meccano had been patented by
Frank Homby as early as 1901, but the construction sets

reached their height of popularity in the 1930s. It is possible
that the 'Trials Book' compiled, probably at that time,
referred to yard number 1071 as *Meccano* because of the
number of times she had been put together and taken apart!
    I have been unable to trace what happened to her;
it seems most likely that, as the article states, she was
broken up on completion of the trials.
    'Record' 32 is one of the best yet: I hope that the
colour cover will become a permanent feature. The photo
on page 196 of the launch of *New York City* shows how
narrow the river was opposite Hill's yard : although she
appears to have come to a halt, her stern appears very close
to the opposite bank, as the number of concerned workers
gazing over her poop rails testifies! There also appears to
be a protective lattice of wood baulks attached to her stern
frame: perhaps ships had been known to have struck the
opposite bank before during launching. Carrying out the
launching calculations (of which I have performed a few)
must have been interesting.
TONY SMYTHE, 35 Avondale Road Rayleigh Essex SS6 8NJ

Tuillier serendipity
Serendipity is the word that usually accompanies reading
'Record' and the latest issue was no exception. The letter
from Colin Menzies entitled 'Thoughts on Tuillier' was the
trigger on this occasion. Sebastiano Tuillier's purchase of a
number of ex-Paddy Henderson ships over the period 1962-
1967 brought mixed reactions amongst Elder Dempster's
seafarers. Their continued employment in the West African
trade satisfied the suspicions of the conspiracy theorists
who were convinced that some in Elder Dempster's
management retained a financial interest in their operation.
Colin's letter blows that theory away. Most of us, despite
worries about the first signs of a decreasing size of fleet,
were glad to see the back of Paddy's 'K' boats. They were
the sort of ships that backed up the image of the Glasgow
shipowner at his most parsimonious. The wooden
wheelhouse of the former *Koyan* is admired in your caption.
This was, of course, highly desirable when your only
compasses were magnetic ones! And I wouldn't mind
betting it might have been acquired second hand by the
yard: the steam cargo winches on the *Kabala* and *Kaduna*
certainly were. So, thanks for the memories. We had some
penny-pinching Chief Stewards in Elder Dempster who
would just serve you half a kipper at breakfast (full fish were
reserved for dinner entrees) but only Paddy Henderson's
people would try and get away with quartered portions.
How much fish do you find on the port or starboard after
quarters of the average kipper?
JOHN GOBLE, 55 Shanklin Road, Southampton SO15 7RG

Henderson s motor ship *Kabala*, which John Goble believes had second hand winches. Built by Lithgows in 1958, she
probably ran in Elder, Dempster colours throughout her British flag career. Sold in 1973, she was renamed *Papamaurice*,
and lasted until broken up at Kaohsiung in 1980. *[Roy Fenton collection]*

City of Barcelona on fire

Looking through 'Record' 19 the photographs of the *City of Barcelona* on page 181 took me back to the days of 1942 when I was a cadet on *Talma* and at the time in the Alexandra Dock, Bombay. The *City of Barcelona* lay at the opposite side of the dock discharging, I think, ammonium nitrate in wooden boxes. In the middle of the afternoon smoke was seen coming from number 4 hold and very soon great clouds of smoke and flames rose into the air. It was not long before explosions occurred in this hold and enormous mushrooms of burning material were forced into the sky. In time some of this burning material was blown towards our ship; we closed all open hatches and turned on the hoses to extinguish the burning material that started to settle on our decks.

In the meantime the fire on board the *City of Barcelona* continued to rage and before long the fire tracked through to number 2 hold and soon the vessel was burning furiously over most of its length. Frequent explosions ejected more flaming material into the sky and we prepared to shift ship, but where to? We continued to hose down and managed to prevent the fire from taking hold of our ship. Eventually the fire was extinguished but by then the *City of Barcelona* looked a terrible sight and we thought that she had reached the end of her days. However, in this critical stage of the war heavy lift derricks were in great demand and she was towed away, patched up and her derrick re-rigged and tested but to a lower safe working load, about 100 tons I think it was when next we saw her at work. This fire may account for the disparity in the two safe working load figures given in your article for her heavy derrick.

Meanwhile the ship ahead of us, the *City of Paris*, was struggling with a bunker fire, moving and discharging some of her steaming coal. Not a happy time for Ellermans.
M.D.A. LEE, 173 Barnes Lane, Sarisbury Green, Southampton SO31 7BH

A lot on little lists

Tony Smythe's comments regarding the stability of timber ships has attracted much interest (page 192 in 'Record 31'), and some corrections to earlier statements appear below. In case you were wondering about metacentre (as were the editors), it is defined as the intersection between a vertical line drawn through the centre of buoyancy of the ship when lying upright, and a vertical line drawn through its centre of buoyancy when it is slightly heeled. The centre of gravity must be below the metacentre so that there is a righting moment when the ship is heeled.

There is a reluctance to write 'Last words on lists', the editorial code for 'This correspondence is closed', but can much more can be written on the subject without getting into higher realms of naval architecture?

Tony Smythe writes:
I agree that a ship with an angle of loll is not in fact unstable, just uncomfortable. However, the suggestion that filling a double bottom tank to help matters can very often make things worse. As soon as the tank begins to fill the free surface effect of the liquid will reduce the ship's stability until the tank is fully pressed up, and matters would often be better left as they were. Captain Kinghorn's letter makes the point about the danger of slack tanks. Having said all this, the photo of *Walkure* at Barry on page 169 of *Record* 31 shows her to have shed her timber deck cargo - was this a direct cause of her accident?
TONY SMYTHE, 35 Avondale Road, Rayleigh, Essex SS6 8NJ

J.A. Douglas wrote about lists and lolls way back in 'Record' 4 (pages 254-5). John Goble's letter in 'Record' 32 (page 218) prompted him to comment further.
In his second paragraph, John Goble says 'Fortunately the position of the metacentre will fall as the vessel heels'. In fact, the metacentre rises as the vessel heels.

Later he says 'either a double bottom tank should be filled on the low side or cargo jettisoned from the high side'.

This is the correct initial action to take, but it does not maximise the righting levers. If either action is taken, the ship will still be heeled, but for a different reason. The centre of gravity will have been lowered, but will be off centre, and the ship has a list as distinct from its earlier loll. It can be brought upright by filling the double bottom tank on the high side, or by jettisoning cargo from the low side. Either action will move the centre of gravity back to the centreline and lower it further, making the ship stable in the upright position.

There are sound reasons for this two-stage procedure. It is imperative that nothing should be done which would cause the centre of gravity to move to the high side of the centreline. If the high side tank was filled first, the ship would come upright, but would immediately lurch to the other side. The momentum of the lurch could cause mayhem and put the ship into a worse position than it was originally, if indeed it recovered at all!
J.A. DOUGLAS, 105 Essex Drive, Glasgow G14 9LX

John Goble responds by pleading guilty as charged to the first correction, but asks for mercy on the second count.
The metacentre must of course rise and I cannot believe, on rereading my letter, how I allowed such a howler to pass my pen. On the second charge I think that Mr Douglas is being a little harsh so I'll plead good intentions that could be misinterpreted. What I tried to do was explain, without getting overly technical, that the best levers use the minimum of weight to gain effect and this means acting over the maximum distance. Hence the adding or losing of weight from what seems to be the wrong places. And I can still recall that the real righting lever was called GZ.

The only timber I carried on deck was logs from West Africa and in that area the problems arose from stowing and securing rather than stability. As I recall from studying for examinations, the actual location of the metacentre in a ship is at a height above the keel that is not very far above the waterline (whereas in the textbook pages, for clarity, it appeared to be on the mast crosstree!). So it was patently obvious that a thousand tons of logs on deck was only a feasible lift if the lower holds had a few thousand tons of copper ingots to stiffen the ship up beforehand. The Greek and Italian ships we saw with logs on deck up to wheelhouse height were either more cavalier about their stability or must have arrived at Mediterranean ports in a very tender (or lolled!) state. Which all goes to support the point that my letter to 'Record' hoped to make. Timber ships with a heavy list were not unstable or unevenly stowed. They had made a very commercial freight maximising decision and then lived thereafter with their lolled state rather than trying to correct it by losing cargo or fouling fuel tanks.
JOHN GOBLE, 55 Shanklin Road, Southampton SO15 7RG

Notes from British Columbia

Having recently acquired some of the early issues of 'Record' (excellent reading), this stone is intended for a small flock of birds (in the interests of accuracy, not pedantry!).
'Record' 3. *Riversdale* page 165. The bow and stern sections of this hulk are still plainly visible in the breakwater at Royston, Vancouver Island, as also are the remains of the former Heap's clipper *Melanope* ('Record' 4, page 238).
'Record' 4. *Ditton*, page 214. While of lesser tonnage, the *Bremen* and *New York*, at 328 feet long, were longer three-masted ships. They were built in 1855 as auxiliary steamers to inaugurate the Norddeutcher Lloyd service between Bremen and New York; acquired by Edward Bates, Liverpool in 1874 and converted into full-rigged ships. I believe they were the longest sailing ships afloat between 1875 and 1887. In 1887 and subsequently a number of longer ships were built, but all had more than three masts. Similar to the *Lancing* ('Record' 6), these ships had a very stubby bowsprit and an abbreviated jib-boom. The foremast was a good 60 feet abaft the stem and at least three headsails could be set. The *Bremen* was wrecked near San Francisco in 1882, the *New York* in Le Maire Strait in 1891.

'Record' 6. *Wanliu*, page 123. I think these are unlikely to be horse boxes - both locations are out of reach of the derricks. Also the box right aft would experience maximum pitching, while that on the fiddly would experience maximum rolling - both unsatisfactory locations for livestock; valuable horses would be kept low and away from the ends of the ship to minimise motion.

'Record' 7. *Severus*, page 170. The stockless anchor is typical of 1894; White Star Line introduced the stockless anchor to their ships in the early 1890s. This ship is surely one of the last so rigged; interesting is the very long lead to all the braces.

Jessie, page 170. The structure would appear to be a pole compass - an effort to reduce the influence of adjacent iron or steel structures. White Star Line's 'big four' the *Cedric, Celtic, Baltic* and *Adriatic* of the early 1900s experienced similar problems. The standard compass was mounted on a pedestal at the fore end of the accommodation, midway between the mainmast and forward funnel. A catwalk connected to the wheelhouse, and presumably a voice pipe too for comparison with the steering compass (and copper and brass to keep the bridge boys occupied).

Hubbock, page 168. Yes, these are lighthouses for the sidelights. Many latter day sailing ships had a similar arrangement, and the steamship *Buteshire*, page 135, is similarly equipped. The *Pluton*, page 167, would certainly have benefited from such a rig. Today, some very large container ships have their sidelights at the break of the forecastle or part way along the fore deck, plus having their deck lights on at sea.

'Record' 9. *Drumrock*, page 30. The ship gave her name to the rock on which she was wrecked. In the early 1970s part of the hull and one lower mast was still perched on the rock but has since disappeared.

Drumeltan, page 32. Note is made of the ship being wrecked on Tanega Shima in 1894. On 22nd November 1998 a monument commemorating the wreck and rescue of the crew was erected at Maenohama, Tanega Shima.

Captain JOHN M. ANDERSON, 523 Louise Road, Ladysmith, British Columbia V9G 1W7, Canada.

Arising from Arosa

Anthony Cooke and Laurence Dunn wrote a remarkable essay on the Arosa Line in 'Record' 31. The origins of Arosa Line and its first Atlantic ship, the *Arosa Kulm*, make for fascinating reading. There are, however, some facts and dates that should be rectified.

1) Nicolo Rizzi was a Swiss citizen residing in Geneva. He grew up on the island of Lucciupiccolo which was awarded to Yugoslavia after the Second World War.

2) The maiden voyage of the *Arosa Sun* was from Trieste on 14th July 1955, arriving Quebec on 6th August. According to the log kept by Achille Donda, New York (on 1st August) was a port of call like Naples and Genoa.

3) I do not think that the *Arosa Sun* limped to Baltimore on one engine in March 1958. Although the first press reports mentioned that port, she probably limped to Savannah or Mobile. Her log for 10th May 1958 indicates a departure from Savannah bound for Bremerhaven. On 12th May she picked up passengers in New York. No mention of Baltimore.

4) The *Arosa Star* was seized in St. George's (not Hamilton) on 7th December 1958. She had sailed from Port-au-Prince and was on her way to New York.

5) The *Arosa Sky/Bianca C.* caught fire on 22nd October 1961. She sank two days later.

6) Regarding the shrinking tonnage of the *Arosa Sun* from 20,126 to 16,231 gross tons, I would appreciate knowing which method was used to determine it. The last tonnage given for *Felix Roussel* in 1954 was 17,083.

I hope Anthony Cooke and Laurence Dunn will continue to produce more of these interesting time capsules.

MICHAEL VON KIRVAN-PICHETTE, Villarosa, 16 rue des chenes sud, Sainte-Petronille, Ile d'Orleans, Quebec G0A 4C0, CANADA

Anthony Cooke responds as follows:

1) I am very grateful to Michael Von Kirvan-Pichette for his kind remarks and particularly for solving the mystery of Nicolo Rizzi's origins. I would just correct him on two very small points: Lussinpiccolo (note the spelling) was actually a village on the Adriatic island of Lussin, which was Italian between the wars. It later passed to Yugoslavia and the names were changed slightly. Incidentally, Lussinpiccolo was one of those small communities which were well-known for producing ship's captains and owners. Most notably, the Cosulich and Martinolich families originated there, although they eventually moved to Trieste.

2) He is quite right in stating that the *Arosa Sun* proceeded to Quebec after calling at New York on her maiden voyage in July-August 1955. Mea culpa.

3) I can, however, confirm that I was correct in saying that the *Arosa Sun* was repaired at Baltimore after her fire in 1958. 'Lloyd's Voyage Records' shew that she was in Baltimore from the 13th April until the 3rd May. She then sailed to Savannah for a 5-day round trip to the Bahamas before leaving Savannah for New York on the 10th.

4) The report I have seen of the arrest of the *Arosa Star* was posted from Hamilton and did not mention St. George's but it may have happened there.

5) There is some confusion over the date when the *Bianca C.* caught fire. The Italian sources which I consulted consistently give it as the 23rd October, 1961 but Lloyd's give it as the 22nd.

ANTHONY COOKE, Unit 212, Station House, 49 Greenwich High Road, London SE10 8JL.

Brown and Simons

The statement on page 60 of 'Record 33' is incorrect in that Andrew Brown was not a naval architect but a mechanical/ marine engineer. He served an apprenticeship with John Neilson, Clydebank Forge, Glasgow, and after various posts as a draughtsman, engine designer and engineer manager, became a partner with William Simons in 1860, later became sole owner, and continued to work at the Renfrew yard until a few days before his death in 1907.

IAN RAMSAY, 'Garmoyle', Main Road, Langbank, Renfrewshire PA14 6XP

SOURCES AND ACKNOWLEDGEMENTS

We thank all who gave permission for their photographs to be used, and for help in finding photographs we are particularly grateful to Tony Smith, Jim McFaul and David Whiteside of the World Ship Photo Library; to Ian Farquhar, F.W. Hawks, Peter Newall, Ivor Rooke, William Schell, George Scott; and to David Hodge and Bob Todd of the National Maritime Museum, and other museums and institutions listed.

Research sources included the *Registers* of William Schell and Tony Starke, *Lloyd's Register, Lloyd's Confidential Index, Lloyd's War Losses, Mercantile Navy Lists, Marine News* and *Shipbuilding and Shipping Record.* Use of the facilities of the World Ship Society's Central Record, the Guildhall Library, the Public Record Office and Lloyd's Register of Shipping are gratefully acknowledged, and particular thanks to Dr Malcolm Cooper and Clive Guthrie for research, to Heather Fenton for editorial and indexing work, and Marion Clarkson for accountancy services.

Sailing Tankers – Part 2
For details of the French sailing tankers see: David, Frédéric, 'Le *Quévilly*, pétrolier à voiles', *Chasse-Maréee*, No.86, pages 16-29;

Lacroix, Louis, *Les Derniers Cap-Horniers Français*, Imprimerie S. Pacteau, Luçon, 1940; Picard, Henri, *Marseille et Marine en Bois, 1860-1925*, Michel Schefer, Marseille, 1983; Randier, Jean, *Grands Voiliers Français 1880-1930*, Éditions des Quatre Seigneurs, Grenoble, 1974; Villiers, Alan and Picard, Henri, *The Bounty Ships of France*, Patrick Stephens, London, 1972. Thanks are due to William Kooiman of San Francisco Maritime National Historical Park for information on the *Calcutta* and to Denis Stonham, editor of *Windjammer*, for information on the *Sunlight* and *Rendova*.

Hain in a Hundred
Background material on the company and its ships is from K.J. O'Donoghue and H.S. Appleyard, *Hain of St Ives*, World Ship Society, Kendal, 1986. Voyage information, including casualty information, is from *Lloyd's List*, while details of shareholdings come from closed vessel registers in BT 110, and wound-up company files in BT 31. Information on masters' careers is taken from the Lloyd's Captains Registers at the Guildhall Library, while crew data comes from the collection of Crew Agreements held at the Memorial University of Newfoundland.

UNDER THE STAR AND CRESCENT:
BRITISH-BUILT SHIPS OWNED IN PAKISTAN - Part 1.
Peter Myers

Pakistan once had a sizeable merchant fleet, which reached its peak at the end of 1971, just before East Pakistan became Bangladesh. Ten shipping companies operated 74 ships and employed 2,200 seafarers. Many of the ships traded between the west and east wings of Pakistan. The country's shipping industry was nationalised on 1st January 1974 and became the Pakistan Shipping Corporation. Five years later, on 1st January 1979, the PSC was merged with the National Shipping Corporation to form the Pakistan National Shipping Corporation and which today remains the country's sole shipowner.

During its formative years, the Pakistan merchant fleet was comprised mainly of second-hand tonnage, which was mostly of British origin. Among the first ships of the East and West Steamship Co., established in 1946, was the *Firoza* of 1913. Other cargo steamers of a similar vintage bought by Pakistani companies were the *Kaderbaksh,* of the United

Oriental Steamship Co. Ltd., and the *Safina-e-Tariq,* of the Pan-Islamic Steamship Co. Ltd., both built at Sunderland in 1918 and both C type standard ships of the First World War. Former British India Line ships of the I class, built during the Second World War, were popular purchases among Karachi shipowners in the 1950s. As steamships became uneconomic, Pakistani shipping companies turned to motor ships and made some shrewd acquisitions on the second-hand market. Some of them gave longer service under the Pakistan flag than under the Red Ensign, most notably the *Safina-e-Ismail* (24 years) and the *Safina-e-Haider* (23 years) of the Pan-Islamic Steamship Co. Ltd. More than half-a-dozen ships have been built for Pakistani owners in Sunderland yards. The last were the SD18 trio of *Ayubia, Kaghan and Murree,* built in 1981 by Austin and Pickersgill Ltd. for the Pakistan National Shipping Corporation.

FIROZA
Ropner and Sons Ltd., Stockton; 1913, 4,729gt, 392 feet
T. 3-cyl built by Blair and Co. Ltd., Stockton
The *Firoza* was one of the first ships acquired by the East and West Steamship Co., a partnership company set up by the Cowasjee family of Karachi in August 1946, a year before British India was partitioned. Despite her age she was suitable for trading along the Indian coast and was joined in 1948 by three former Royal Indian Navy 'Basset' class naval trawlers which were converted to cargo

ships. Cowasjee and Sons had been established as stevedores and shipping agents at Karachi since 1883 before venturing into shipowning. The *Firoza* had been built as the *Falls City* as seen above for the Bradford Steamship Co. Ltd., managed by William Reardon Smith. On 22nd January 1916, the *Falls City* was damaged by a mine south from Kentish Knock, and to save the ship her master had beached her. There were no casualties and after repairs she was returned to service. She was transferred to the St. Just Steamship Co. Ltd. in 1917 and later to the Reardon Smith Line Ltd. in 1928. A year

later the *Falls City* was sold to the South Georgia Co. Ltd. (Christian Salvesen and Company), Leith, and renamed *Seringa.* She retained her name when she was bought by the Claymore Shipping Co. Ltd., Cardiff in 1939 and survived the Second World War to be sold in 1945 to the Basra Steam Shipping Co. Ltd. (Galbraith, Pembroke and Co. Ltd.), London, who in turn sold her to the East and West Steamship Co. She was sold for breaking up at Gadani Beach in October 1960. *[David Whiteside collection]*

SAFINA-E-TARIQ

J. Blumer and Co. Ltd., Sunderland; 1918, 3,323gt, 331 feet
T. 3-cyl by J. Dickinson and Son Ltd., Palmer's Hill, Sunderland.

The Pan-Islamic Steamship Co. Ltd. was incorporated on 4th March 1950 and had Arab investors. They were well-known for their pilgrim ships, which were featured in 'Record' 9, but they also operated cargo ships and among the first was the steamer *Safina-e-Tariq*. She had been completed as the C-type standard ship *War Coppice* during the First World War for the Shipping Controller. She became the *Nord* in 1919 and then the *Refrigerant* in 1920, before being bought by the United Baltic Corporation Ltd., London, and renamed *Baltraffic* as seen right. After the Pan-Islamic bought her in 1951 and renamed her *Safina-e-Tariq*, the company acquired a more modern cargo ship the following year in the form of the twin-screw Japanese ship *Tsukushi Maru* (8,135gt/1941) which became the *Safina-e-Millat*. The *Safina-e-Tariq* was sold for breaking up at Karachi in January 1957. *[Ships in Focus]*

KADERBAKSH

J. Blumer and Co. Ltd., Sunderland; 1919, 3,071gt, 331 feet
T. 3-cyl by J. Dickinson and Son Ltd., Palmer's Hill, Sunderland.

The *Kaderbaksh* was one of the first ships of the United Oriental Steamship Co., Karachi, which was a partnership company set up by Maula and Iqbal Baksh and their brothers, who came to Karachi from Chiniot in the Punjab. She

had been laid down in 1919 as the *War Planet*, a C type standard cargo ship, for the Shipping Controller, and was completed as the *Cyprian Prince* for the Prince Line Ltd. as seen below. She was renamed *Moorish Prince* in 1936 and later that year was sold to the Bristol City Line who renamed her *Gloucester City*. In November 1940 her crew distinguished themselves in rescuing 92 survivors from four ships from the famous *Jervis Bay* convoy that had been attacked by the German pocket battleship *Admiral Scheer*. After the war she became the *Namaqualand* of South African Lines in 1949 before being acquired by United

Oriental in 1951. She arrived at Gadani Beach, 37 miles along the coast from Karachi, in December 1961 for demolition. *[Nautical Photo Agency/J. & M. Clarkson collection]*

FATAKADA/MINOCHER COWASJEE

Irvine's Shipbuilding and Dry Docks Co. Ltd., West Hartlepool; 1921, 5,415gt, 420 feet
Three steam turbines by Richardsons, Westgarth and Co. Ltd., Hartlepool.

The East and West Steamship Co. added this ship to their expanding fleet in January 1949 and named her *Fatakada*. She had been built as the *Parisiana* for

Neptune Steam Navigation Co. Ltd.
(Furness, Withy and Co. Ltd., managers),
London, but after only a year her name
was changed to *London Exchange* in 1922.
She was on the London-Philadelphia-New
York service for many years, and one of
her former crew members, writing in 'Sea
Breezes', said that in spite of the hard
weather on the North Atlantic run, 'there
was no better-maintained or cleaner ship
sailing out of London'. However, her mate
was described as a taskmaster and her
seamen and apprentices dubbed her the
'Labour Exchange'. In 1934 she was
transferred to Johnston Warren Lines Ltd.,
and in November 1938 she was sold to the
Ben Line of Leith, and became their
Benrinnes (right). The East and West
Steamship Co. changed her name from
Fatakada (middle) to *Minocher Cowasjee*
in 1955, but she was to have a tragic end.
On 21st December 1956, she sailed from
Dairen, China, for Antwerp. She was
reported south-east of Mauritius on 24th
January 1957 but thereafter disappeared.
*[Top: J. & M. Clarkson collection,
middle: G. A. Osbon/World Ship Society
Limited]*

MUSTALI (1)
*Lithgows Ltd., Port Glasgow; 1921,
4,500gt, 385 feet*
*T. 3-cyl by Rankin and Blackmore,
Glasgow*
The *Mustali* was one of two former Clan
Line ships to end their days under Karachi
ownership. She was built as the *Clan
Maciver* and gave 20 years' service for The
Clan Line Steamers Ltd. (below) before she
was sold in 1951 to Compagnie Maritima
S.A., Costa Rica, and renamed *Carrena*.
Just two years later she was bought by
Gulf Steamships Ltd., Karachi, and

renamed *Mustali*. Her new owners had
been established in May 1948 as a private
limited company and the *Mustali* served
them until 1961 when she was sold to
Pakistani breakers. *[B. & A. Feilden/J. &
M. Clarkson]*

FIRDAUSA
*Furness Shipbuilding Co. Ltd., Haverton
Hill-on-Tees; 1923, 7,938gt, 472 feet*
*Two single-reduction geared turbines by
John Brown and Co. Ltd., Clydebank.*
The *Firdausa* had had an interesting
history before she was bought by the East

and West Steamship Co. in 1949, and which is fully related in the article 'The Furness Goalposters' in 'Record' 17. She was built as the *London Importer* for Furness, Withy, and in 1933 was sold to the Admiralty, becoming the Royal Fleet Auxiliary *Reliant* (right). After wartime service in the Mediterranean and the Indian Ocean, the Ministry of Transport sold her to Maltese owners in 1948 and she was renamed *Anthony G.* East and West got 14 years' service from the *Firdausa* before she was broken up in 1963 at Gadani Beach. *[Tom Adams collection]*

FAKIRJEE COWASJEE

Furness Shipbuilding Co. Ltd., Haverton Hill-on-Tees; 1925; 5,342gt, 418 feet T. 3-cyl. by Richardsons, Westgarth and Co. Ltd., Hartlepool.

This ship was built as the *Manchester Commerce* for Manchester Liners and served on her owners' trans-Atlantic cargo services from Manchester to Canada and the east coast of the United States (right). During the Second World War she carried military supplies in support of the Allied campaign in North Africa and in 1944 spent much of that year ferrying mules from South Africa to India. In 1952 she was sold to Camel Lines and renamed *Corbita*, but later that year she was sold to the East and West Steamship Co. of Karachi, and renamed *Fakirjee Cowasjee* (below). After 15 years' trading she was sold for demolition by Pakistani breakers in 1967. *[Middle: B. & A. Feilden/J. & M. Clarkson, bottom: Ships in Focus]*

OCEAN ENDURANCE (1)/OCEAN ENDEAVOUR

*Sir James Laing and Sons Ltd.,
Sunderland; 1940, 5,199gt, 454 feet
T.3-cyl. by Richardsons, Westgarth and
Co. Ltd., Hartlepool*

The *Ocean Endurance* was acquired in
1954 by the Trans-Oceanic Steamship Co.
Ltd. of Karachi, which was originally a
private limited company set up by the
Dinshaw family, headed by Nadirshaw
Eduljee Dinshaw. She had been built as the
Charlton Hall for Charles G. Dunn
Shipping Co. Ltd., Liverpool. In 1944, she
became the *St Elwyn* of the Shakespear
Shipping Co. Ltd., Cardiff (top, with the

Royal Navy tug *Sprite* alongside), before
being transferred to the South American
Saint Line Ltd. in 1951. Trans-Oceanic
bought her in 1954, renaming her *Ocean
Endurance* (middle, May 1955). She was
renamed *Ocean Endeavour* in 1966 to
make way for the second *Ocean
Endurance* (q.v.), also built at Sunderland.
The *Ocean Endeavour* was broken up in
1967. *[Top: Tom Rayner/J. & M.
Clarkson, middle: J. & M. Clarkson]*

CHITTAGONG CITY

*Furness Shipbuilding Co. Ltd., Haverton
Hill-on-Tees; 1940, 5,136gt, 416 feet
T. 3-cyl. by North Eastern Marine
Engineering (1938) Co. Ltd., Newcastle.*

The Dinshaws were also the principal
shareholders of the Chittagong Steamship
Corporation, of Chittagong, East Pakistan,
who began trading with the *Chittagong
City,* bought in 1958 (right). She had
previously been the *Madras City* of the
Reardon Smith Line Ltd. Her sister ship,

the *Orient City* (5,095gt/1940), also built
by Furness, was also sold to Pakistani
owners that year, becoming the *Feronia* of
the East and West Steamship Co. The
Feronia was broken up in 1970 at Gadani
Beach while the *Chittagong City* followed

a year later. After Bangladesh became
independent in 1971, the Chittagong
Steamship Corporation moved its
registered office from Chittagong to
Karachi. *[Ships in Focus]*

[To be continued]